LEADER'S GUIDE K-8 **SU**

Sharable Parables

FAITH ALIVE
Christian Resources

Grand Rapids, Michigan

Any questions or comments about this unit?
We'd love to hear from you:

Faith Alive Christian Resources
1-800-333-8300
E-mail: editors@faithaliveresources.org

RCA Children's Ministry Office
1-800-968-3943
E-mail: childrensministry@rca.org

Presbyterians for Renewal
1-502-425-4630
E-mail: office@pfrenewal.org

Walk With Me curriculum has been developed by Faith Alive Christian Resources in cooperation with the Children's Ministry Office of the Reformed Church in America and with Presbyterians for Renewal.

We are grateful to Roger Groenboom, Alison Groenboom, and Susan Thornell for their work in developing this summer unit of *Walk With Me*. We are also grateful to Margo Burian for drawing the diagrams for this unit.

Unless otherwise indicated, the Scripture quotations in this publication are from the HOLY BIBLE, NEW INTERNATIONAL VERSION, © 1973, 1978, 1984, International Bible Society. Used by permission of Zondervan Bible Publishers.

Walk With Me
Kindergarten-grade 8
Summer, Book 1: Sharable Parables

Faith Alive Christian Resources published by CRC Publications.
© 2004 by CRC Publications, 2850 Kalamazoo Ave. SE, Grand Rapids, MI 49560. All rights reserved. Printed in the United States of America on recycled paper.

www.WalkWithMeOnline.org

ISBN 1-59255-176-9

10 9 8 7 6 5 4 3 2 1

Contents

How to Use This Book 4
Tailoring Your Sessions to the Ways Children Learn 8
A Summer Celebration Program 9
Additional Program Ideas 10
Session 1: The Sower and the Seed
              Large Group Session 12
              Small Group Session, K-3 16
              Small Group Session, 4-8 26
Session 2: The Wise and Foolish Builders
              Large Group Session 36
              Small Group Session, K-3 40
              Small Group Session, 4-8 50
Session 3: The Great Banquet
              Large Group Session 58
              Small Group Session, K-3 62
              Small Group Session, 4-8 70
Session 4: The Lost Son
              Large Group Session 82
              Small Group Session, K-3 86
              Small Group Session, 4-8 96
Session 5: The Good Samaritan
              Large Group Session 106
              Small Group Session, K-3 110
              Small Group Session, 4-8 120
Dramas 131
Songs 153
Reproducible Pages 179
Leader's Evaluation 223

How to Use This Book

"Therefore everyone who hears these words of mine and puts them into practice is like a wise man who built his house on the rock."

—Matthew 7:24

Jesus often spoke to people using parables. The five parables in this course are stories that Jesus told to teach people about the kingdom of God. From them we also can learn about God's kingdom, and we can share these parables with others. That's why we call them "sharable parables."

Goal and Theme

The unique format of this five-session course allows you to use it as a lively and exciting curriculum for your summer church school or for an entire week of summer ministry programs such as vacation Bible school (see pp. 6-7 for helpful tips).

Whether you choose a church school or summer ministry setting, the goal of this course is to teach children five of the parables that Jesus told. We pray that leaders, kids, and all who participate in the sessions and in the summer celebration program will come to know more about Jesus. To help meet this goal, one main theme will shine brightly throughout the session plans: God wants us to share these parables and the good news of Jesus Christ with everyone—not just family and friends, but everyone! We need to hear the words of Jesus and put them into practice.

To support our theme, this book offers a variety of ideas and options for large group sessions, small group sessions, and a summer celebration program. Use the ideas and options that work best with your church school or summer ministry. Ideally, the large group session takes about 15-20 minutes, after which kids break into their small group sessions for 30-40 minutes. You may also want to schedule an extra practice time or two if your church is planning on hosting the summer celebration program.

Finding time to do everything in this book will not be possible—or even desirable—for most churches. You'll need to choose what your group will be able to handle in the time you have available. Be sure to purchase one copy of this book for each of your leaders. As purchaser of this book, you are granted permission to photocopy the dramas, patterns, and activities on reproducible pages 131-152 and 179-221.

Getting Started

Because these materials suggest a different format and approach than the regular *Walk With Me* units, you'll want to spend some extra time planning and preparing. Athough each church situation is unique, you may find some of the following suggestions helpful:

- In early spring, organize a small team to read through this book. These folks can review the session plans, dramas, and songs, then choose what they think will work best for your church.

- After the committee makes its recommendations, recruit teachers, song leaders, accompanists, and drama participants.

- Recruit volunteers who are willing to gather materials for these special sessions. Give them plenty of time for this task (a month or two) since they will likely want to ask the congregation to save and/or gather some of the items.

- Schedule rehearsals for the drama team.

- If you're planning to use the summer celebration program, schedule a single, final rehearsal for everyone involved in the program.

Large Group Sessions and Summer Celebration Program

The large group session materials include a drama for each week and a list of songs to learn as a whole group. Presenting a drama may, at first, sound intimidating, but these dramas are written in such a way that both children and adults will enjoy performing and/or viewing them. Each drama will take about 8-10 minutes, and each requires five to eight actors (more actors are optional). The costumes may be as simple or elaborate as you would like.

You'll probably want middle schoolers or a team of older teens to play these roles (although adults would be fine too). Each drama offers ways to include younger children in nonspeaking roles, if you wish. Please see session 1 for more information.

The dramas and songs can be used not only for each large group session, but also for the celebration program. You'll find a sample program along with ideas for organizing and producing it on pages 9-11.

Small Group Sessions

Small group sessions will give you the opportunity to help apply the story to the children's lives. If you are unable to present the story as a drama in the large group setting, you can still use the drama to tell the story another way in your small group setting. It's a story you want children to hear!

Each small group opens with a Hello step designed to catch the children's interest and get them thinking about the lesson's theme.

Next comes the Know step (telling the story). If the children have already heard the story in the large group session, you'll want to use this time to review the story with them. If they did not participate in a large group session, you can use the drama or another interesting way to present the story to the group (see sessions for suggestions).

The Grow step will help kids understand what the story means for their lives, and the Show step will guide them to respond to what they learned in this session.

Each small group session includes options for activities and crafts. You'll want to carefully consider these well ahead of teaching these materials. Once you've decided which crafts and activities to use, you may want to appoint two or more volunteers (possibly parents of kids in the group) to gather the materials, cut out patterns, and assemble all the items you'll need. Having a helper in the classroom is also a plus when doing crafts and other activities with young children.

We trust that God will use you as you share these parables of the kingdom and the love of King Jesus with the children.

> **tip** Small group leaders may want to send a short letter to the families of the kids in their group at the beginning of this unit. Explain what these five sessions will be like and invite families to share in the experience by praying for you, talking about the stories with their kids, helping out in your sessions, and/or attending the final celebration program (if you plan to have one).

How to Use This Book for VBS or Other Summer Ministries

Much of this material was originally written for vacation Bible school at Westview Christian Reformed Church, Grand Rapids, Michigan, by Rev. Roger Groenboom, Alison Groenboom, and Susan Thornell. You can use the five sessions for a five-day vacation Bible school, as the authors did, or for a once-a-week session for five weeks. Here's a suggested schedule and format for using the large and small group approach for vacation Bible school.

Opening Large Group Session (30 minutes)

- Opening prayer and singing time (Check each session for song suggestions; all are included on the CD that accompanies this course.)
- Drama (See pages 131-152 for dramas for each of the sessions and tips on how to present them. Purchasers of this book may photocopy all drama scripts.)

Small Group Sessions (45-90 minutes)

Small groups may spend 90 minutes or more enjoying the four steps of the session plans. Remember that you'll need to make some choices about what to use and what to ignore, especially in the Show part of each session.

- The Hello step (10 minutes) gets you started with a fun activity that introduces the theme of the parable.
- The Know step (10-15 minutes) gives you some great ways to review the parable that was presented in the large group session.
- The Grow step (10-15 minutes) helps nurture faith as kids think about how the parable affects their lives.
- The Show step (15-30 minutes or more) helps kids respond to the parable through a variety of crafts and activities. You'll find suggestions for learning the Memory Fun or Memory Challenge, making attractive parable bookmarks, and retelling the parable to others. You'll also find single session ideas for parable-sharing crafts, fun projects, and other activities.

Closing Large Group Session (15 minutes)

You may want to get the entire VBS back together for a time of singing and sharing. If you're planning a summer celebration program, you can use this time to review the songs that are part of the program. Kids can recite their memory work and show their crafts or other projects to the entire group. End your time together by inviting everyone to join hands for prayer.

> **Terrific Tees**
>
> Westview Church makes the summer program extra-special for staff and kids each year by ordering T-shirts printed with the program logo for all participants. (See p. 179 for a "Sharable Parables" logo that can be screenprinted onto shirts or printed on a program.) When ordered in large quantities, these T-shirts are quite inexpensive. Look for a printer in your area.

Forming Ministry Teams

Sharable Parables provides a great opportunity for many people from your congregation to become involved in summer outreach ministry. Here are a few suggestions for setting up teams from your congregation:

- Planning team: Decides the dates of the program. Assists and guides the other teams so that the main theme and vision of the VBS or other outreach program is apparent.
- Music team: Chooses music, finds music leader and musicians, selects music for program. This material suggests a number of songs and includes them on a CD.
- Publicity team: Creates small fliers and distributes them throughout the neighborhood. Gets the word out about location, date, and theme.
- Program team: Organizes the celebration program and possibly an "after-program" event like an ice cream social or small picnic.
- Small group session team: Selects the ideas that will be used for the small group sessions, especially for craft and activity time.
- Drama team: Recruits actors, obtains the necessary items for each drama, and presents the drama to the entire VBS. See session 1 for additional comments.
- Decoration team: Decorates the large group session area as desired, perhaps with large drawings of the characters in the parables (use an overhead projector to trace onto shelf paper), enlarged Memory Fun/Memory Challenge verses and Sharable Parables logo, and so on.

We encourage you to draw on the diverse gifts of members when you compose your teams. Involve as many people from the congregation as you can. Share your enthusiasm about the parables and how the children will respond to them with others!

Tailoring Your Sessions to the Ways Children Learn

How do children and young teens learn? The answer to that question can be almost as varied as the kids in your group. Some learn best through words. Others through music. Still others through nature or through movement.

Sessions in the *Walk With Me* curriculum try to respect the many ways kids learn. *Walk With Me* sessions include a wide range of activities that speak to kids with the following types of intelligence (based on Howard Gardner's theory of multiple intelligences). Within each session, the icons below highlight the learning styles represented by each activity. As you teach, you'll begin to get a sense for how the kids in your group learn best. Kids who are

 Word Smart

learn best through verbal activities (listening, reading, or speaking), including discussions, worksheets, writing, reading, storytelling, and word games.

 Number Smart

learn best by exploring patterns and relationships through activities such as problem solving, logical puzzles or games, making charts and graphs, or putting things in sequence.

 Picture Smart

learn best by visualizing concepts. These kids enjoy viewing maps, slides, pictures, videos, and diagrams; making jigsaw puzzles; and expressing their ideas with shape, color, and design.

 Body Smart

learn best by using their bodies, acting things out, using puppets, moving—anything hands-on.

 Music Smart

learn best through sound, music, and rhythm—playing musical instruments, writing their own songs and raps, listening to recordings, singing, and so on.

 People Smart

learn best through doing things with others, cooperating and working in small or large groups, role playing, conversations, brainstorming, and other interactive exercises.

 Self Smart

learn best by working independently through such things as writing in a journal, meditating, reading, and reflecting.

 Earth Smart

learn best through activities connected to living things and natural phenomena, through nature walks, examining plants and animals, nature experiments, and activities that focus on ecology.

—The ideas on this page are based on material from the following resources: *Multiple Intelligences in the Classroom* by Thomas Armstrong, © 2000, and a chart prepared by Donald L. Griggs, Livermore, California.

A Summer Celebration Program
Sharable Parables

Processional and Greeting: *"Ha La La La" (David Graham)*

Opening Prayer

Reading: *The Sower and the Seeds (Matthew 13:3-8)*

Song: *"Stop and Let Me Tell You"*

Memory Fun (younger children)
Psalm 119:105

Memory Challenge (older kids)
The Wise and Foolish Builders (Matthew 7:25-27)

Song: *"He Is the Rock" (Troy and Genie Nilsson)*

Reading: *The Great Banquet (Luke 14:21b-23)*

Song: *"Big House" (Mark Stuart, Barry Blair, Will McGinnis, Bob Herdman)*

Congregational Song: *"Amazing Grace" (John Newton, arr. Thomas A. Arne)*

Drama: *"The Lost Son" (Luke 15:11-32)*

Song: *"Amazing Grace/Fill It Up" (Grooters and Beal)*

Reading: *The Good Samaritan (Luke 10: 30-37*

Song: *"Jesu, Jesu" (Ghana folk song, adapted Tom Colvin, arr. Robert Roth)*

Meditation

Closing Prayer

Additional Program Ideas

Having a summer celebration program is a great way to help focus your church's attention on sharing the good news about Jesus. This program can be used during a Sunday service or for a special weeknight "bring-a-neighbor" service. Read through the sample program (previous page) and use it as a guide for creating your own unique program. (You may want to use the logo on p. 179 for a program cover.)

Here are a few additional ideas:

Scripture Readings
- Your middlers and younger children who are good readers can nicely present this part of the program. Consider using simplifed English versions such as the New International Reader's Version or the New Living Bible. *The Message* could also be used for one or two of the readings.

- Children can recite their Memory Fun/Memory Challenge in unison. Note that the younger children learn a different passage than the older ones. Both are given opportunity to recite in the program.

Singing
- We suggest six songs for the children to sing during the program (the audience sings "Amazing Grace" just before the dramatization of the Lost Son). All the songs the children sing are on the CD that's part of this resource, as are the optional songs you may want to substitute, below. Even if the children know all the songs by the last session, you may still want to plan an extra practice session, perhaps on a Saturday or evening. Having a closing song time during your weekly or daily sessions will also give the kids time to practice the songs.

- You may want divide up the songs. For example, kids in K-3 could learn a few of the songs while kids in the other grades learn the rest. For the program, have each group sing the songs they've learned, instead of having all the kids sing together. Or have boys learn some songs and girls learn others.

- If kids make the paint stick clappers in session 2, use them during the singing of "He Is the Rock," "Amazing Grace/Fill It Up," and "Jesu, Jesu." See pages 47-48 for instructions on making the clappers.

Drama
- Presenting one of the dramas from this course is bound to delight your audience. We suggest using the drama of the Lost Son (see pp. 145-148). You could omit reading the entire Scripture passage for that drama, reading instead only the "lost and found" reference from Luke 15:31. Of course, if you think one of the other dramas would be more effective, feel free to substitute.

- The drama can be presented by your drama team or by other adults, young adults, and middle schoolers. Involve younger children in nonspeaking roles. Costumes, props, and sets can be as simple or elaborate as you like. Read through the suggestions at the beginning of each drama.

Stage Direction Ideas for the Program
- **Pre-processional:** Have the children line up in the back of church.

- **Processional:** All of the children enter the worship space from the back of church singing "Ha La La La." Encourage the children to smile and greet people as they enter. They can shake hands with each other and with the people in the congregation.

- **Formation up front:** Line kids up in front. They can be spread across the front of the worship space in a single row or several rows. (During practice time, assign each child a special spot or area where they will be standing when they sing during the program.)
- **Singing:** If you are planning on having all of the kids sing all of the songs, they may all stay up in front of church. If smaller groups are singing certain songs, have the others stay seated until it is their turn to sing.
- **Opening Prayer:** Have one of the older kids open with prayer. He or she can thank God for the Bible and the parables that they are going to share, as well as ask God's blessing on the program.
- **Scripture Reading:** Have kids that are reading move to a visible location. Microphones may or may not be necessary depending on the size of your worship space.
- **Transition to Drama:** After kids sing "He Is the Rock," have them exit the worship space to make room for the drama or have them sit down. During the transition time, have the accompanist play music.
- **Drama:** The drama team will need to set up and take down quickly. They may need some extra stagehands to help them. Sets and props do not have to be elaborate; perhaps they can be partially set up ahead of time. Have the accompanist play music during the transition time before and after the drama.
- **Transition to Meditation:** Following the song "Jesu, Jesu," the children should be seated. The pastor then leads the balance of the worship time.

Optional Songs

Feel free to substitute some of the following songs for those suggested for the program. These optional songs are listed in the large group sessions and are printed at the back of this manual. They're also on the CD that accompanies this course.

- "Tell It!" (Cindy Berry)
- "The Wise Man and Foolish Man" (traditional)
- "Two Houses"(Robert C. Evans)
- "Sandy Land" (Karen Lafferty)
- "The Good Samaritan" (Mary Lu Walker, arr. H. Myron Braun)
- "You Shall Love the Lord" (Frank Hernandez)
- "Make Me a Servant" (Kelly Willard)

Large Group Session
The Sower and the Seed

Scripture
Matthew 13:3-8, 18-23

Focus
Jesus teaches us to keep telling others about him because many will believe.

WORDSearch

Think About It
In the parable of the sower and the seed, we meet a farmer and his seeds. Quickly we are navigated through the neighborhoods where the seed falls. Some seed falls along a path, but the birds eat the seed. Other seed falls on rocky places, but the sun withers the seed. Still more seed falls among thorns, but the thorns choke out the seed.

"How sad," we are tempted to think. This is one bad-aim farmer. He's like a hunter with a bent sight. And by the way, what a waste! All that seed, and not a single stalk to show for it. We object to his promiscuous planting. It's as wasteful as throwing away a pint of pure nard (John 12:3). Unfortunately, this whole seeding enterprise seems to be going to the dogs (make that the birds!).

But then, these infertile side streets are not the parable's final destination. There's one more borough to visit—the good soil. Arriving there, we realize that Jesus' words have brought us to a place designed to make us forget all the failures. It's like that family vacation where everything goes wrong—a flat tire on the camper, a Freon leak turning your climate-controlled Chevy into an oven on wheels, and Junior's dreadful nausea, complete with not-so-special effects. But none of that wretchedness matters when you round the bend, and there is the Grand Canyon in all its majesty. Or the Tetons, or Lake Louise, or wherever your favorite place may be.

"Forget about the failures," the farmer is telling us. "Other seed fell on good soil, where it produced a crop a hundred, sixty, or thirty times what was sown." We've arrived at last at a place where the soil is right, the shade brings relief, the birds are in retreat, the thorns are removed, and the seed is ready. *Everything*, in fact, is ready. Everything is ripe for a superabundant harvest. This is our destination on the kingdom tour. Do you see it off in the distance?

But wait, that's only part of the story. That's just the ending. As every traveler knows, even with the flat tires, Freon leaks, and flu symptoms, the journey itself holds a special satisfaction of its own. Not to mention the fact that on the journey is exactly where we find ourselves.

Pray About It
This is a parable about a superabundant harvest in the kingdom of God. Pray that you will be a part of God's promiscuous seed-sowing project. Pray that the children will understand the message of good news, and that it needs to be told again and again to others, especially to those who have never heard. Pray for opportunities to share some seeds with your students and others. Pray for the courage and boldness to live with the promise of an assured multiplying harvest. Pray that God's harvest will increase through your voice telling out the good news.

Tell About It
The children need to hear that the fields are ripe for harvest. They need you to tell them about the joy of sharing the good news. They need to know that God will bless the gospel message they learn and tell. They need to know that thirty-, sixty- or even one hundred-fold is easy for God, even when it looks and feels so difficult for us. They need to know that we should speak the good news with confidence, for many will believe it.

And right there on the journey is where we need to hear a couple of companion verses to our parable. The first (John 4:35) is spoken by Jesus to his disciples: "Do you not say, 'Four months more and then the harvest'? I tell you, open your eyes and look at the fields! They are ripe for harvest."

Do you see the connection? The harvest is ripe *right now*. We are all on a harvest journey—a journey on which everyone we meet who hasn't heard the good news should be considered an opportunity. God has ripened the fields, and we are walking through them. Shall we walk right on by or shall we gather the harvest by opening our mouths with the words of good news? Surely God has provided the opportunity.

God has also given us a promise. We hear it in a companion verse. Can you guess what it is? "My word that goes out from my mouth . . . will not return to me empty, but will accomplish what I desire and achieve the purpose for which I sent it" (Isa. 55:11). There we have the promise: a harvest of achievement, a harvest of accomplishment, a harvest of fullness. The Word of God will go out on the voices of God's people and the harvest will be gathered.

Both opportunity and promise abound even today in this 21st century. Dear teacher of children, we are on the journey of our lives. So let's take our feet off the brakes and honk our horns telling out God's goodness; and then let's sow the good news far and wide, confident that the Holy Spirit will awaken the superabundant harvest.

Planning the Session

You are in charge of presenting the parable of the sower to all the children—from kindergarten to grade 8—in your Sunday school or vacation Bible school. That's quite a challenge! The little ones on your group will hear the parable as an interesting (and somewhat funny) story about a farmer and seeds. Older kids, at least those familiar with Scripture, may already begin making some connections between the seed and the gospel. Here in the large group session, you should concentrate on presenting a lively and interesting story for all to enjoy; interpretation of that story will happen in the small groups.

Depending on how much time you have available, you'll probably want to take 5-10 minutes for singing and another 10-15 minutes for the drama.

If you're going to be presenting a summer celebration program, you may want to use part of the large group session to help the children prepare. You'll find suggestions for program planning on pages 9-11.

The suggestions in this large group session assume that you'll be dramatizing the parable of the sower to children and young teens and preparing them to respond to it in small groups.

Singing

You may want to ask someone with musical gifts to lead the singing and teach new songs to the children during these five sessions. Be sure to share the tips in the box "Introducing a New Song" with that person.

You'll find the songs on pages 153-178 of this book and on the CD that accompanies this course. A great warm-up song that will get everyone involved is "Ha La La La." A song that relates directly to today's parable is "Stop and Let Me Tell You." Both are suggested for the summer celebration program.

An optional song for this session or for the entire unit is "Tell It!" by Cindy Berry.

If you decide to present a summer celebration program, consider dividing the songs between groups of children: the children in kindergarten-grade 3 might learn some of the easier songs, those in grades 4-8 could sing all of the songs.

Introducing a New Song

The way you introduce a new song is crucial. Of course you'll want to know it well yourself. But you'll also want to think through how you'll introduce it to your group. Here are a few ideas to keep in mind:

- Many kids learn mostly by rote and repetition. Listen to the CD or play the tune and encourage the kids to join in on a line or phrase that repeats often.
- Make up motions that may go along with simple words (i.e. step, Jesus) to help them remember the words.
- Be enthusiastic! Model your love of singing instead of being concerned about your performance.

Drama

Rehearsing and presenting a drama can be a rewarding experience—both for the actors and for those who view the drama. Consider finding a team of actors and begin working with them early. This could be a wonderful gift for your middle school group to offer to the younger children. Teens and adults can also be drama team members. And children of all ages can play nonspeaking roles. This week's drama, "The Sower and the Seeds," includes seven reading parts plus as many nonspeaking parts for the "Good Seeds" as you can line up—the more, the better! You'll also want to begin thinking about costumes and props—consider asking persons in the congregation (especially people who sew!) to help you out.

> **tip** Roger Groenboom, author of the dramas in this course and pastor of Westview Christian Reformed Church, where this material was taught in a VBS setting, says kids enjoyed watching their pastor and other teens and adults acting in the skits. "They especially enjoyed it when I goofed up the lines," says Roger. He said the team managed to "loosely" memorize their lines, improvising a bit as they went along. On the weekend before VBS began, the team rehearsed the first two dramas. Once VBS was underway, they rehearsed and learned lines in the evening. To cut down on the time required from drama team members, consider forming two or more drama teams.
>
> If your drama team doesn't have time to memorize, reading the lines from scripts you provide is fine. Drama teams can still rehearse together, even though they aren't memorizing their lines.

Simple costumes are suggested on the first page of the script. The suggestions we offer are only that—suggestions. Use what you have available and what you can find to create your own costumes. The most important prop is plenty of tan or brown sheets (burlap sacks would also work). Put out an early call for these! A few rocks and small branches are simple enough to collect.

> **tip** No time or people for drama teams? Present the dramas without rehearsal, choosing your actors from the large group, distributing costumes and scripts, and walking your actors through the presentation. It won't be smooth, but it's certainly doable. You'll need to allow more time than for rehearsed performances by a drama team. Plan to have at least one adult "stage manager" who gets kids assigned to parts, distributes costumes, and, when necessary, acts as a prompter to keep the action moving. It would also help to have an older teen or an adult—perhaps a small group leader—take a major role in the play. For this week's drama, get an adult to play the farmer.

Please note that two pieces in the skit have been set to music by author Roger Groenboom (both are sung by him on the CD). The first, "I Am a Little Seed" (p. 135; CD, track 3) may be sung by the Road Seed. The second, "The Money Song" (no printed music available; CD, track 4) may be sung by the Choked Seed. This song, says Roger, is "loosely based" on the Veggie Tales "Bunny" song from the video *Rack, Shack, and Benny: A Lesson in Handling Peer Pressure.*

Before presenting "The Sower and the Seeds," ask someone—preferably a good reader from your middle school—to read the parable from Matthew 13:3-8; 18-23, using an easy-to-understand version such as the New International Reader's Version (NIrV). A careful, slow reading will help children understand what the drama is about.

Small Groups

After the drama, children will meet in small groups. Notice that we've included two session plans—one for kindergarten-grade 3 and another for grades 4-8. If your regular church school leaders are present, it's probably best to have the children meet in their groups as usual; however, you could also choose to combine several groups together. Each small group leader will need to adapt the plan to the needs of his or her children.

Small Group Session: Kindergarten-Grade 3

1 The Sower and the Seed

Scripture
Matthew 13:3-8, 18-23

Memory Fun
Psalm 119:105

Focus
Jesus teaches us to keep telling others about him because many will believe.

1 HELLO — Taste and Guess
Body Smart
Earth Smart

Goal
Think about seeds and what they become when they grow.
Time
10 minutes
Materials
☐ Small pieces of a variety of fruit and veggies on toothpicks (watermelon, apple, tomato, cucumber, carrot, beans, and so on)
☐ Platter or large plate to hold fruit and veggies
☐ Blindfold
☐ Seeds from a couple of the fruits or veggies

When all the children are present, remind them that today's Bible story is about seeds and the fruit or veggies that grow from them. Show them the plate of fruit and veggies on toothpicks and explain that they're going to have a chance to see how good they are at identifying what they're eating.

Invite kids to come forward, one at a time, put on the blindfold, choose an item, taste it, and tell what they think they just ate (be sure to observe what item they took so you can tell if they guessed correctly). Enjoy the game and applaud everyone, whether they guessed correctly or not.

tip: Before proceeding, ask if any of the children are allergic to any fruits or vegetables. If so, remove the offending items from your platter!

After all have had a chance to guess, show the group seeds of a couple of the fruits and vegetables you've brought. Let them guess what kind of seeds they are. Ask them to imagine that they are farmers. Would they plant just one seed if they wanted, say, one watermelon, or would they plant many seeds? Conclude that we would want to plant more than one seed because some seeds may not sprout.

time saver: No time to find a variety of fruits and veggies? Then stick to just one fruit and its seeds. Let's say it's watermelon. Show the group the watermelon seeds without identifying what fruit they'll grow into. Ask the kids to close their eyes as you place a piece of watermelon in their mouths (or have one volunteer do the guessing). Can they identify the fruit without looking at it? Transition to today's topic with comments like those that conclude the regular step.

2 KNOW
Today's Parable Retold

Picture Smart · Earth Smart · Word Smart

Goal
Retell the parable of the sower and the seeds.

Time
10 minutes

Materials
☐ Plastic tablecloth—solid color is better than patterned
☐ Small pile of dirt
☐ A couple of large and small rocks
☐ Branches/brambles
☐ Piece of tan/gray felt for a path
☐ Bowl of grass seed or other seed
☐ Cap or straw hat

Spread out your props and put on your hat. Ask the children to imagine that you are a farmer who is going to sow some seeds. Alert them to be ready for four questions you're going to ask. Tell them they should respond with a loud YES or NO.

First, sow some seeds along the path. Ask, **Will this seed grow up into beautiful plants?** After the children respond, talk about what happened to those seeds—the birds ate them before they had a chance to grow.

Then sow some seeds by the rocks. Ask, **Will these seeds grow?** Let the children respond, and then talk about what happened to those seeds—because they took root in shallow soil, among the rocks, these seeds grew at first but then withered away in the heat of the sun.

Next, sow some seed among the branches (thorns). Once again, ask, **Will these seeds grow?** Again let the children respond. Talk about what happened to these seeds—the thorns choked them out.

Finally, sow some seed on the good dirt and ask, **Will these seeds grow and produce healthy plants?** After the children respond (at last!) with a loud and enthusiastic YES, talk about how these seeds will grow up into beautiful, strong plants that will provide a lot of food for people to eat.

> **tip** If you have second and third graders in your group, you could ask them to take turns being the farmer and sowing the seed in the various places.

Storybook
Picture Smart · Word Smart

Option to step 2

Time
5-10 minutes

Materials
☐ Storybook, "The Parable of the Sower and the Seeds" (reproducible pages 185-186), copied and assembled

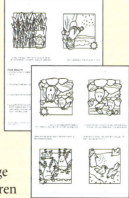

Use this option if you're looking for a simpler way to present today's story. Assemble a sample storybook before class and show the children the pictures as you read through the pages together.

If your photocopy machine has this feature, you may want to enlarge the pages of the storybook to full size, making it easier for the children to see the book as you read it. Or, if you're artistic, copy the simple drawings and text yourself onto full-size pages.

tip: You may want to ask an older child to read the story to the others. If so, try to get a copy of the book to the child before today's session so that he or she can practice reading it at home.

3 GROW
People Poster

- Word Smart
- Picture Smart
- Number Smart
- People Smart

Goal
Sense how important it is to tell others about Jesus.

Time
10–15 minutes

Materials
☐ Several "people pictures" per child (cut from magazines; look for diversity in age, race and so on)
☐ 6' (2 m) length of paper tablecloth or large sheet of posterboard
☐ Glue sticks
☐ Marker

Give a very simple explanation of the parable by reading these lines to the children: **The farmer in the parable sows *many* seeds. The farmer wants as *many* seeds to grow as possible. The farmer wants to have *many* bushels of wheat or corn at harvest time. God also wants *many* people to believe in him, know him, and love him. God wants *many* people to tell others about Jesus. God wants *many* people to be in the kingdom.**

Tell the children you're going to say these same words to them again. This time, whenever you point to them, you want them to jump up like seeds popping from the ground, and shout *many* together. Try this once or twice.

Ask the kids who in the world needs to hear about Jesus (everyone!). That's why it's so important that we tell people about Jesus. Explain that you're going to make a "people poster" together. Distribute several people pictures to each child. (Have these available ahead of time, or, if you prefer, allow extra time and have kids cut out the pictures themselves.)

Roll out about a 6' (2 m) length of paper tablecloth on a table or the floor (or display a large piece of posterboard). Have kids attach their people pictures to the paper or posterboard using glue sticks. As they work, mention the many different kinds of people on the poster, reminding the children again that everyone in the world needs to hear the good news about Jesus.

When they've finished gluing the pictures, ask the group to think of a title for their poster: something like "Tell everyone about Jesus" or "The whole world needs Jesus." You may also want older children to count the number of people displayed on your poster. Ask them to imagine how big their poster would have to be to show a picture of everybody in the whole world!

Conclude by helping the children think of ways that we can share the good news about Jesus. For example, we can talk about Jesus with our friends at school. We can pray for our missionaries. We can be kind and loving to others so they can see if we love Jesus. And we can even "share a parable" that we learned at church school or VBS.

Note: If you make the people poster, please save it for reference later in this unit.

Seed Pictures Picture Smart   Word Smart

Option to step 3

Time
10-15 minutes

Materials
☐ Drawing paper
☐ Crayons or colored markers

Use this option if you prefer a more open-ended art activity to the people poster in the regular step. Begin by giving everyone a seed—watermelon, bean, sunflower, and so on. Talk about the variety of sizes, but do not tell what kind of seeds they are.

> **tip:** Instead of buying seeds in a packet, save money by buying fifteen-bean soup mix.

Distribute drawing paper and crayons or colored markers. Ask kids to use their imagination and draw a picture of what they think their seed might become. This is just for fun—it doesn't matter if the drawing matches the seed! It might be a fruit, a vegetable, even a tree!

When they're finished, admire the sketches, then ask what they think their seed needs to grow up into a plant or tree. Explain that, like the seeds, everyone in the world is different. But everyone needs to know and love God. God wants us—and all people—to grow up to love and serve him. Talk about how we can help others know about God and grow into the kind of people that God wants them to be.

4 SHOW
Show and Tell

Goal
Celebrate and share the good news about Jesus.

Time
15-30 minutes or more

Materials
See individual projects for lists

Like the sower who plants seeds everywhere, we want to tell the good news about Jesus whenever we can. Below are a variety of projects to help kids celebrate and share the good news about Jesus. Some of the projects run for the entire unit, others are for just this session. Choose one or more that best suits your time frame and the interests of your children.

Unit Project Ideas
Memory Fun   Word Smart

Time
5-10 minutes

Materials
☐ Memory Fun (reproducible page 181), one per child

Tell the children that during your times together in the next few sessions, they'll be hearing stories Jesus told called parables. Jesus told these stories because he wanted people to know how to live as God's children.

Read the Memory Fun verse to the children. Then read it again, phrase by phrase, and have the children repeat it after you. Talk a bit about what the verse means. The words and stories Jesus tells are like lamps or lights: they help us see how to live. Urge the children to listen carefully to the stories they will hear during your time together. That's what Jesus wants us to do!

If you plan to have the children memorize this verse, send home a copy of the Memory Fun home today with a note asking families to help the child learn these important words.

Sharable Parable Bookmarks 👁 Picture Smart   AA Word Smart

Time
5-10 minutes
Materials
☐ Bookmark pattern (reproducible page 187), one bookmark per child
☐ Crayons
☐ Construction paper, various colors
☐ Paper punch
☐ Glue sticks
☐ Small pieces of ribbon

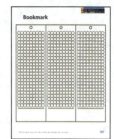

Have the children make bookmarks to share with others the parable they hear each session. Run copies of the pattern (page 187) on heavy stock. Younger children can simply color in the circles to create a picture or design. Older children can glue on paper-punched circles made from various colors of construction paper for a mosaic look. For today's session, a flower or tree or sun and field would make an appropriate design.

Notice that there's room at the bottom of the bookmark to print a title or the Scripture location of the parable. If you are working with very young children, you will want to add that before the session. Attach a ribbon through a hole punched at the top of the bookmark.

Encourage kids to show the bookmark to their families and friends and to share the parable with them.

Storybooks AA Word Smart   👁 Picture Smart   👥 People Smart

Time
15 minutes
Materials
☐ Storybook, "The Sower and the Seeds" (reproducible pages 185-186), one set per child
☐ Crayons or markers

Each of the five sessions offers a take-home storybook that the children may share with their family and friends. For today's session, photocopy pages 185-186 and distribute a set to each child. Walk the children through the folding process, as follows, offering your help and the help of older children to the little ones in your group.

1. Fold both pages in half horizontally along the dotted lines.

2. Fold both pages in half vertically along the dotted lines.

3. Insert the second set of folded pages into the first set, so that page 3 is opposite page 2.

Have the kids print their names on the cover, then color in the pictures. (If you're short on time, just read the booklet with them and let them color it at home.) Encourage them to read the story with their family and friends.

One-Session Project Ideas
Sower and Seed Flowerpots

Earth Smart   Picture Smart   Body Smart

Time
20-30 minutes

Materials
☐ Small clay flowerpots about 2" (5 cm) high, one per child
☐ Plain label stickers, various colors and shapes (available at office supply stores)
☐ Colored pencils, markers, crayons
☐ Scissors
☐ Potting soil and plastic spoons
☐ Cover-up shirts or other protection for children's clothing
☐ Flower seeds such as Zinnia
☐ Masking tape
☐ Video labels
☐ Plastic baggies and rubber bands

Designing their own mini-flowerpots and planting seeds will help kids remember and tell others about the parable of the sower.

Follow these steps:

1. Draw designs on the stickers (discuss ideas before children begin drawing and encourage designs that reflect the story, such as plants, seeds, paths, rocks, birds, sun, and so on). An example is shown below using circle labels.

2. Cut out the designs and stick them around the lower part of the flowerpot.

3. Cut the video labels into long, thin strips so that they fit around the rim of the flowerpot. First have the children write "The Sower and the Seeds" on the label (or write the title on the labels for them before the session).

4. Cover the bottom hole of the pot with a piece of masking tape.

5. Using the plastic spoon, have kids fill each pot with potting soil (provide some "cover-up" shirts or other protection for children's clothing). Then have them plant a few small seeds such as Zinnia seeds.

> **time saver** If your time is quite limited, or if you are working with very young children, you may want to prepare the stickers before the session and have them cut out and ready for the children to stick on their pots. You may even want to decorate the pots ahead of time and just have the children do the planting to complete the project.

6. Cover the pots with plastic baggies and secure them with rubber bands for a dirt-free trip home.

Tell kids to put the pots in a warm, sunny place and to keep the soil moist. (If you are working with very small children, be sure to send a short note home with the plant!) If you planted Zinnia seeds, the plant can be transferred to the garden when it's about five inches tall.

Encourage the children to tell the story of the parable when family members and friends admire their plant.

My Parable Picture of Seeds People Smart   Picture Smart

Time
15 minutes
Materials
☐ 12" x 18" (30 x 45 cm) piece of posterboard, one per child
☐ Variety of seeds
☐ Glue sticks
☐ Crayons or markers

First have the children use crayons or markers to draw the farmer and the various places he planted the seed (you'll need volunteer helpers to work with younger children on this, reminding them of the different types of soil from the parable). Then distribute the seeds and show the children how to glue them to the posterboard. If time permits, let the children use their picture to tell the story to a partner or to you.

Parable Story Box   People Smart

Time
20-30 minutes

Materials
☐ Small shoe box, one per child
☐ Large seeds (such as bean seeds or sunflower seeds)
☐ Very small stones or gravel
☐ Piece of tan felt for the path
☐ Piece of black felt for the dirt
☐ Branch with pretend paper thorns taped on (or small twigs)
☐ Glue sticks (for felt items)
☐ White glue or tacky glue (for seeds)
☐ Pipe cleaners to make farmer-figure

Before the children assemble their story boxes, review with them the various places where the farmer sowed seeds. Show them the various items (stones, tan felt, and so on) that will be used to represent each place in the story box.

Consider walking younger children through the construction of the story box, step by step, handing out an item from your supply pile and waiting until everyone has the item glued down before proceeding to another item. We suggest first gluing down the felt and other items to represent the various places, then adding the seeds. Pipe cleaners can be used to make the figure of the farmer (stand him up by bending the legs to form feet; tape the feet down to the shoe box).

> **time saver** To save time and assist the younger children, have the various pieces of felt cut out prior to your session. Be sure to show the children a finished model of your own parable story box. In addition to finding volunteers to help you gather and prepare materials, you may want a volunteer or two to attend this session and offer assistance to children as needed.
>
> Another timesaving option is to build one story box together as a group.

Older children may prefer to plan their own design for the story box, selecting materials from a supply table and proceeding at their own pace.

Here's a sample of what a finished story box could look like:

> **tip** White glue or craft glue will take some time to dry. Rather than have the children take the boxes home today, let them stand in your classroom or on a closet shelf until your next session.

God's Little Seeds Word Smart Picture Smart

Time
10 minutes

Materials
☐ *God's Little Seeds* by Bijou Le Tord (Eerdmans Publishing Co., 1998)

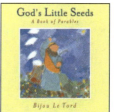

Your group will enjoy this delightful retelling of the parable as well as the lovely watercolor illustrations. The book also includes the parable of the mustard seed.

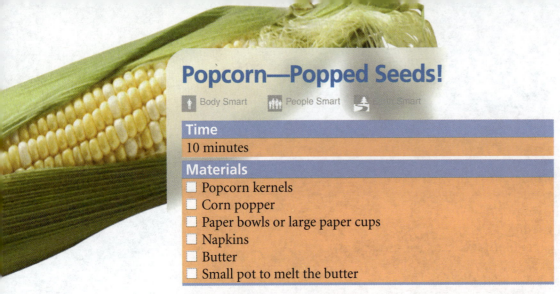

Popcorn—Popped Seeds!

Body Smart   People Smart   Earth Smart

Time
10 minutes

Materials
☐ Popcorn kernels
☐ Corn popper
☐ Paper bowls or large paper cups
☐ Napkins
☐ Butter
☐ Small pot to melt the butter

Show the kids the popcorn kernels and remind them that popcorn is nothing more than popped corn seeds. Have fun making and eating the popcorn together. An alternative, of course, is to buy microwave popcorn (kids can look at some of the unpopped corn kernels left in the bag.

Small Group Session: Grades 4-8

1 The Sower and the Seed

Scripture
Matthew 13:3-8, 18-23

Memory Challenge
During this unit the children may memorize the parable of the wise and foolish builders. Since that parable is told in session 2, it's probably best to introduce the Memory Challenge project at that time.

Focus
Jesus teaches us to keep telling others about him because many will believe.

1 HELLO — Sink That Shot!

Body Smart
Number Smart

Goal
Introduce the parable of the sower.

Time
10 minutes

Materials
☐ Soft balls (such as Nerf or tennis balls)   ☐ Hoop or bucket   ☐ Small bags of popcorn as prizes (optional)   ☐ Lemonade or juice (optional)

Prior to your session, set up a shooting game that involves trying to sink a shot at some target. A wastebasket and some tennis balls would work fine; or maybe you've got a Nerf basketball and hoop at home that you can bring to class. Or just bring pennies to pitch into a cup. Make the shot challenging enough so that kids will miss at least some of their attempts.

When the kids come into your room, tell them they each have three shots at the target. If you want to ham it up a little, pretend that you're running a concession at a fair. "Step right up here, sir. Sink one shot and win a prize!" If you like, offer bags of popcorn to everyone who participates. Tell kids the popcorn is a clue to what today's Bible story is about. If you go the popcorn route, have some lemonade or juice available for thirsty kids.

Ask kids to guess what the overall shooting percentage of the group was: 25 percent of shots taken? Fifty? Seventy-five? Explain that our first "sharable parable" features a farmer who also took some "shots"—and who missed more than a few! He threw out a whole bunch of seeds. Some missed the target, but many made it and grew up into beautiful plants. The parable is called "The Sower and the Seeds." (Does anyone get the connection between the popcorn and the parable? Both are about seeds.)

Taste and Guess

Option to step 1

Time
10 minutes
Materials
☐ Small pieces of a variety of fruit and veggies on toothpicks (watermelon, apple, tomato, cucumber, carrot, beans, and so on)
☐ Platter or large plate to hold fruit and veggies
☐ Blindfold
☐ Seeds from a couple of the fruits or veggies

Try this mouth-watering option if you're more into snacks than games. It's all spelled out for you in the Hello step of the session for K-3 (p. 16). Actually, it's lots of fun for kids of all ages. You can alter it a bit, if you wish, by having kids pair off to do the tasting and guessing (in that case, supply multiple plates of fruits/veggies and multiple blindfolds).

Body Smart
Word Smart

Time
15 minutes
Goal
Retell the parable of the sower and the seeds.
Materials
None needed

A fun way to review today's Bible story (or present it for the first time if you did not have a large group session) is to act out the story in what may be a new way for the kids in your group.

The basic idea is simple and familiar: you will narrate the story from Scripture, a line at a time, while kids act it out. The fun part is that kids play inanimate objects like seeds, rocks, birds, sun, thorns, and so on. So the birds get to eat the seeds that fell on the path; the thorns get to wrap their arms around the seeds that fell among them and pretend to choke them; the sun gets to rise and shine, and so on.

Ask for volunteers for the following:
- the farmer (sower)
- seeds that fell on the path
- birds
- seeds that fell on rocky ground
- the sun
- seeds that fell among thorns
- thorns
- seeds that fell on good soil

 tip If you're thinking this little drama requires a huge group of kids, don't worry. Just assign kids to multiple roles.

Begin by opening your Bible to Matthew 13:3 and reading "Listen! A sower went out to sow . . ." *(kid playing farmer pretends to sow seeds)*

Continue: "As he sowed, some seeds fell on the path . . ." *(kids playing seeds on the path fall down on the path)*

"And the birds came and ate them up." *(kids playing birds begin eating kids playing the seeds on the path)*

And so on, until you finish the parable at verse 9.

After the drama, ask for a volunteer to read Jesus' explanation of the parable from Matthew 13:18-23. Then ask: **What do you think Jesus is teaching us in this parable?** Focus on two basic responses:

- We need to allow God's Word to take root and to grow in us so that we become strong, healthy Christians—just like the seed needs good soil to grow into a healthy, productive plant.
- We need to tell others the good news so that as many people as possible come into God's kingdom.

3 GROW
Good Seeds Dramas

Body Smart
Word Smart

Time
15 minutes
Goal
Describe how we can help "sow the seed" of the good news about Jesus.
Materials
None needed

Say something like this: **This parable is a picture of the way people are saved and the way God's kingdom grows and grows. Jesus is saying that even though some seeds landed on bad ground, many other seeds landed on good ground. A huge, healthy crop of new believers is coming! But listen—we are the ones who must tell others about Jesus. We are the ones to spread the good news in our neighborhood, at school, wherever we are, however we can.**

Divide into small groups of 3-5 kids, taking care to have younger and older children in each group. Ask the groups to demonstrate—act out or pantomime—two or three things they could do in their neighborhood, at school, at church, and elsewhere to help spread the good news about Jesus. Give them five minutes or so to come up with ideas, then let the groups make their presentations. Here are some possible actions they could demonstrate:

- Pray for a missionary in your church; write him or her a note.
- Share a parable with a younger child (see ideas in the next section of this lesson).
- Do something kind for someone who is not a Christian.
- Don't be ashamed to let kids at school see you pray or read your Bible.
- Use language that's appropriate for a Christian; avoid profanity or dirty talk.
- Invite someone at school to attend your youth group at church.
- Talk with friends and others about what Jesus means to you.
- Donate some of your time to work in a food pantry or similar project.
- If people ask why you go to church or pray, tell them you do that because you love Jesus.

Commend the groups for all their ideas.

Where Am I in This Parable?

Self Smart   Body Smart   Word Smart

Option to step 3

Time
10 minutes

Goal
Reflect on where we are in this parable.

Materials
☐ "Where Am I in This Parable?" (reproducible page 189), one per person
☐ Pen or pencil

Use this option if you want to try a more personal approach to the parable of the sower and if your kids enjoy writing. Distribute a copy of reproducible page 189 to each person. Read the sentence starters to the kids and ask them to think about which response or responses they'd like to check and then complete with their personal thoughts.

Allow five minutes for writing, then invite any who wish to share any or all of their statements to do so. You may want to ask all the kids to suggest ways we can be more like the farmer, spreading the good news about Jesus.

Conclude this step by having a time of silent prayer, during which each person may talk to God about what he or she wrote. Open and close the prayer yourself.

4 SHOW
Sharing the Good News

Goal
Celebrate and share the good news about Jesus.

Time
15-30 minutes or more

Materials
See individual projects for lists

Like the sower who plants seeds everywhere, we want to tell the good news about Jesus whenever we can. Below are a variety of projects to help kids celebrate and share the good news about Jesus. Some of the projects are for the entire unit of five sessions; others are for just this session. Choose one or more that best suits your time frame and the interests of your kids.

Unit Project Ideas
Sharable Parable Bookmarks Picture Smart   Word Smart

Time
5-10 minutes
Materials
☐ Bookmark pattern (reproducible page 187), one bookmark per person
☐ Crayons
☐ Construction paper, various colors
☐ Paper punch
☐ Glue sticks
☐ Small pieces of ribbon

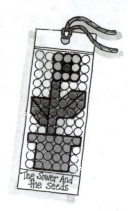

Have group members make bookmarks to share with others the parable they hear each session. Run copies of the pattern (see page 187) on heavy stock. Kids can either color the circles to make a design or they can glue on paper-punched construction paper circles of various colors for a circular mosaic look.

For today's session, a flower or tree or sun and field would make an appropriate design. Notice that there's room at the bottom of the bookmark to print a title or the Scripture location. Attach a ribbon to the bookmark through a hole punched at the top.

Sun Art Picture Smart   Earth Smart

Time
15-20 minutes
Materials
☐ Construction paper in various dark colors
☐ Removable glue sticks (check your local craft store)
☐ Scissors
☐ Large seeds
☐ Pen

This project, adapted from a Martha Stewart newspaper column, uses the power of the sun to make a unique kind of art. Kids can make interesting illustrations related to the parables they're learning. You could do this project for one session or for all five, depending on the interest of the kids and your time schedule.

The basic idea is to place cutout shapes on a sheet of colored construction paper. Cut shapes from construction paper, and glue them with removable glue to the sheet. Then tape the sheet, cutouts facing out, to a window where it will catch a lot of sun. After a week or so (longer if higher contrast is desired), peel off the cutouts. The images will be bold and sharp on the construction paper, while the paper surrounding the images has faded in color.

For today's session on the parable of the sower, kids could make cutouts of flowers, stems, and leaves to glue on their construction paper. Or they could make a cutout of the farmer and glue seeds to the construction paper around him (any relatively flat object placed on the paper will make a sharp outline). Letters can also be used as cutouts for those who want to label their artwork.

Kids can take this project home today, hang it in a sunny window, and let the sun do its work for a week or so. Encourage them to show their art to their family and friends and explain how it relates to the parable of the sower.

One-Session Project Ideas
Parable Story Box Earth Smart   Picture Smart   People Smart

Time
20-30 minutes
Materials
☐ Small shoe box, one per person
☐ Large seeds (such as bean seeds or sunflower seeds)
☐ Very small stones or gravel
☐ Tan felt for the path
☐ Black felt for the dirt
☐ Branch with paper thorns taped on (or small twigs)
☐ Glue sticks (for felt items)
☐ White glue or tacky glue (for gluing seeds)
☐ Blue construction paper (to represent the sky)
☐ Pipe cleaners to make farmer-figure
☐ Scissors
☐ Masking tape

These story boxes will be fun for the kids to make as gifts for younger children in their family or neighborhood. They would also be great to take to a babysitting job.

 tip If you are working with middle school kids, you may want to help a group of younger children make these boxes. Check with Kindergarten-grade 1 leaders to see if they'd appreciate your group's help!

Before kids assemble their story boxes, review with them the various places the farmer sowed the seeds. Show them the various items (stones, tan felt, and so on) that will be used to represent each place in the story box. Place all the supplies on a table where kids can readily locate them. Have scissors available for cutting out the various pieces of felt. You may want to show them a finished model of the story box (see below), but encourage kids to use their own designs for the boxes and to plan out their design before gluing down the various pieces.

Suggest that they may first want to glue down the felt and other materials, then add the seeds. Pipe cleaners can be used to make the figure of the farmer (stand him up by bending the legs to form feet; tape the feet down to the shoe box).

 tip White glue or craft glue will take some time to dry. Let the boxes stand in your classroom or on a closet shelf until your next session.

Here's a sample of what a finished story box could look like:

31

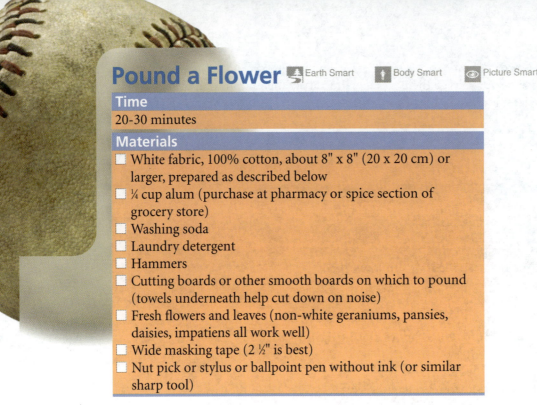

Pound a Flower 🌲 Earth Smart   👤 Body Smart   👁 Picture Smart

Time
20-30 minutes

Materials
- ☐ White fabric, 100% cotton, about 8" x 8" (20 x 20 cm) or larger, prepared as described below
- ☐ ¼ cup alum (purchase at pharmacy or spice section of grocery store)
- ☐ Washing soda
- ☐ Laundry detergent
- ☐ Hammers
- ☐ Cutting boards or other smooth boards on which to pound (towels underneath help cut down on noise)
- ☐ Fresh flowers and leaves (non-white geraniums, pansies, daisies, impatiens all work well)
- ☐ Wide masking tape (2 ½" is best)
- ☐ Nut pick or stylus or ballpoint pen without ink (or similar sharp tool)

Here's a fun project that requires some preparation at home prior to your session but pays off in a unique and attractive piece of flower art that should delight your kids. The final product can be displayed as a wall hanging or, if made small enough, used as a beautiful bookmark. If you line up a volunteer to help you with the preparation, the rest is a piece of cake (make that a bed of roses).

Either buy fabric pretreated for dyeing (available at some fabric stores) or prepare your own as follows:

- Wash fabric in hot water and laundry detergent. Add two tablespoons of washing soda per yard of fabric. Run the fabric through a double rinse cycle to make sure the soda has been removed.
- Pour two cups of hot water and ¼ cup alum (per yard of fabric) into a pail. Stir well and add fabric. Add more hot water if needed to cover fabric. Allow to cool for two hours.
- In a separate bowl, mix a teaspoon of washing soda per yard of fabric with about ½ cup of water. Stir into the bucket of fabric.
- Soak for at least eight hours, then rinse well, wring out, and partially dry on a line (not in dryer). Iron until wrinkle-free.

That's the hard part. Now for the fun part:

1. Cut fabric into squares of at least 8" (20 cm) each if you want the final product to be a wall hanging. If you want to make bookmarks, cut the fabric into bookmark size (approximately 2 ½" x 8" or 6 x 20 cm).

2. Select a fresh flower, removing a few petals for larger flowers. Leaves are also great. Place the flower or leaf on the fabric, face down. Apply wide masking tape over the entire flower or leaf, covering it completely. To add definition, trace around the edges of the flower with a nut pick or other sharp pointed tool.

3. Turn fabric over, place it on a cutting board with a towel underneath the board, and begin to pound the taped areas gently but firmly with a hammer. You'll notice the color begin to emerge right away. Continue until you're happy with the look.

4. Turn fabric over and remove tape and smashed flower. Let dry for a minute or two, then add to your flower arrangement until complete.

5. Display the finished piece as a wall hanging (or use as a bookmark, if you made the smaller piece).

It's probably best to show your kids the entire process, then let them try a practice flower on a small piece of fabric. Once they see how the process works, they can begin on the regular-sized fabric. Encourage them to talk about the parable of the sower as they show their finished art to their families.

Class Story Picture — Picture Smart, Word Smart, People Smart

Time
15 minutes
Materials
☐ 6'-8' (2-2.5 m) length of paper tablecloth (check your church kitchen)
☐ Markers, crayons, in various colors

Unfurl a roll of paper tablecloth that's long enough for everyone in the class to work on simultaneously (you may want to use two rolls if your group is larger than ten). Place the paper tablecloth on a table or on the floor.

Have kids work individually or in pairs to illustrate the parable of the sower. They can use their Bibles to decide which kids will draw what story scene. A sample arrangement:

- One person/pair can begin at one end of the paper and sketch the farmer sowing seeds.
- The next person/pair can sketch birds gobbling up seed from the path.
- The next person/pair can show small plants in rocky soil being scorched by the sun.
- The next person/pair can show plants being choked out by thorns.
- The final person/pair can show healthy plants producing a huge crop. The sower is smiling.

The class can add a caption to the finished product and display it for the congregation to enjoy.

Greenhouse Field Trip   Earth Smart   People Smart

Time
1-2 hours
Materials
☐ Signed permission slips from kids' families
☐ Transportation to a nearby greenhouse
☐ Arrangements with greenhouse owner

Perhaps there is someone in your congregation or community who owns a greenhouse and who would be willing to give your group a guided tour, showing kids how he or she raises plants to sell from the seeding process right through the sale itself. He or she could also talk about some of the different types and sizes of seeds, the care that seedlings require, some of the "thorns" that the plants have to fight to survive, and the fun and reward of seeing everything grow. If the owner of the greenhouse is a Christian, ask him or her to make some ties to the parable of the sower.

Before you make the arrangements, talk it up a bit with your kids. See if they're interested. If they are, make your contacts, arrange for permission from parents and for transportation, and go "greenhousing." Who knows, your brief field trip might just help produce a future farmer (or maybe a future pastor!). And it will make the parable come alive for everyone.

Large Group Session
The Wise and Foolish Builders

Scripture
Matthew 7:24-27

Focus
Jesus teaches us to build our lives on him by obeying him.

WORD Search

Think About It

The parable of the wise and foolish builders sits like a fork in the road at the end of Jesus' Sermon on the Mount. After Jesus finishes his preaching and teaching on how to live a righteous life, he hits us with two simple alternatives: either build your life on my teaching or don't. Choose the former and your house stands tall; choose the latter, and when the tough times come, your house will fall. The options are clear and simple.

Clear and simple. We can all understand this word picture Jesus paints. A house on a *rock* foundation may be harder to build and it may not be in the prettiest location, but it finishes strong. A house on a *sand* foundation may be easier to build but won't survive the storm. The choices are clearly laid out. You sit at this fork, and down one prong you see a beautiful house sitting on a rock. Down the other prong, sooner or later, you see nothing but rubble. No surprises. No guesswork involved. Jesus gives two choices, and he gives two results. All that remains is how the hearer or the reader will answer Jesus' implied question: "How will you build? Will you build wisely or foolishly?"

The obvious answer, of course, is to build wisely. For we know the rock-solid outcome of the wise alternative. But why else? Why else should we follow the wise prong at the fork in the road? First of all, we can trust the one who teaches us how to live. After all, the speaker here is Jesus. Jesus has just preached the beatitudes; Jesus has educated us about being salt and light in this world; Jesus has just given a "how to fulfill the law" tutorial on, among other things, murder, adultery, divorce, retaliation, benevolence, prayer, money and worry. Jesus then says, "Whoever hears these words *of mine . . .*" Note the emphasis here. These are none other than Jesus' words. The words of the Way, the Truth and the Life. These are trustworthy instructions on living. For they come from the Trustworthy One—these words of *mine*.

But again, what other reasons do we have for building on the rock? Let's take a walk back to the Old Testament and Psalm 62:5-7, where David says: "Find rest, O my soul, in God alone; my hope comes from him. He alone is my rock and my salvation; he is my fortress, I will not be shaken. My salvation and my honor depend on God; he is my mighty rock, my refuge." God himself, you see, is David's rock. God is the Rock, the

Pray About It

Pray that Jesus' teaching will begin to really hit home in your life. Pray that the words of Jesus will begin to move from your ears to your heart and out to your hands and mouth. Pray that the children you teach will also build on the Rock and live in the house that features obedience in every room.

Tell About It

Tell the children that the choices they make every day have everything to do with what kind of spiritual house (life with Jesus) they are building. Every decision, every thought, every word, every deed is either going to be built on the rock or on the sand. And what's built on the rock will stand firm. For the Rock is Jesus. We build on Jesus the Rock by learning what he says and doing what he teaches.

never-failing refuge. Build on him and you will not be shaken, even when the tough times come as hard and as fast as they did for David.

Now return to the New Testament, 1 Peter 2:4-8: "As you come to him, the living Stone [a reference to Jesus], you also, like living stones, are being built into a spiritual house. . . . The one who trusts in him will never be put to shame. . . . Now to you who believe, this stone [Jesus] is precious. But to those who do not believe . . . 'A stone that causes men to stumble and a rock that makes them fall.' They stumble because they disobey the message. . . ."

Where are we going with this? Turn to one more text, John 14:31. Jesus, speaking to his disciples, says, "The world must learn that I love the Father and that I do exactly what my Father has commanded me." And that's precisely what we're looking for. Does Jesus himself practice what he preaches? The answer is yes. The Rock who is Jesus, the living Stone, builds on the Rock who is God, that is, David's and our refuge and fortress. The Son of God does exactly what his Father commands. The Son obeys the Father. Rock builds on Rock. Jesus takes his very own sermon to heart. How much more should we?

If you need one more reason to build a life of obedience on the Rock, turn to Mark 6. Jesus enters his hometown, starts to teach, and the people are amazed. They exclaim: "Isn't this the carpenter?" (v. 3). Jesus, of all things, is a carpenter. And from this carpenter comes a story about two men who built houses. . . .

Planning the Session

Having had one large group session, you probably have a clearer idea of how much time you can spend on singing and how much on the drama. If you're planning on presenting the summer celebration program, you may want to budget some extra time for singing so that children can review the songs from last week and learn the new songs for this session.

The suggestions in this large group session assume that you'll be dramatizing the parable of the two builders to children and young teens and preparing them to respond to it in small groups.

Singing

As kids enter, play the song "Ha La La La" from the CD (track 1). Invite the kids to join you in singing this fun action song. You may also want to review "Stop and Let Me Tell You" (track 2). Both songs are included in the summer celebration program.

The new song suggested for today's session (and for the program) is "He Is the Rock" (track 5). An alternative (or second song) is the traditional "The Wise Man and the Foolish Man" (track 6).

Two optional songs for this session are "Two Houses" (track 13) and "Sandy Land" (track 14).

Drama

Before presenting today's drama "The Wise and Foolish Builders," ask someone—preferably a good reader in middle school—to read the parable from Matthew 7:24-27, using an easy-to-understand version such as the NIrV or New Living Bible.

To present the drama you'll need the script on pages 137-140 and seven readers. Please see session 1 for general comments regarding drama teams, memorizing lines, and presenting the drama without rehearsal.

Today's set has two basic areas: one for the Rocky Mountain Builders and one for the Sandland Builders. Props are simple construction tools (trowels, hammers, saws) and a variety of beach items (pails, shovels, surfboards, and so on). Please see the drama itself for

> **tip** You can easily add nonspeaking roles to the drama by having younger children be construction workers for Rocky Mountain Builders or Sandland Builders. They can pretend to be working away as Rob conducts his interview of the two builders.

specific suggestions. To make your task easier, elicit help in collecting these items from members of your congregation.

Dress your Rocky Mountain Builders in plastic hard hats, if possible. Tool belts and/or nail aprons are also a nice touch.

Note that the drama can begin with theme music. Either use one of the songs on the CD (we suggest the traditional "The Wise Man and the Foolish Man" because it will probably be familiar to some kids and most leaders), or arrange for live music (piano, guitar, and so on).

Perhaps your production will be a rehearsed presentation by a drama team of teens and adults, complete with a cool set and lots of props. Or maybe you're winging it with a few props and an unrehearsed reader's theater approach. Either way, your kids should enjoy this skit's humor and exaggerated characters.

Small Groups

After the drama, children will again meet in small groups. Notice that we've included two session plans—one for children in kindergarten-grade 3 and another for children in grades 4-8. If your regular church school leaders are present, it's probably best to have the children meet in their groups as usual; however, you could also choose to combine several groups together. Each small group leader will need to adapt the plan to the needs of his or her children.

> **tip** Before today's session, it's a good idea to ask your leaders how it went last time. How did kids respond? Did they have enough time? Were they able to find necessary materials? Did they have enough room? Be sure they understand that they do not need to use all the ideas in their lessons (many are optional). Use their comments to make adjustments in schedule, rooms, supplies, number of helpers, and so on.

Small Group Session: Kindergarten-Grade 3

The Wise and Foolish Builders

Scripture
Matthew 7:24-27

Memory Fun
Psalm 119:105

Focus
Jesus teaches us to build our lives on him by obeying him.

1 HELLO
Body Smart People Smart Number Smart

Game: Let's Build a House

Goal
Have fun and prepare for the Bible story.
Time
10 minutes
Materials
☐ Many small paper or plastic cups ☐ Tape measure

Divide into teams of three to five kids. Place the paper cups where the teams can easily reach them (or divide the cups up among the groups). Explain that each team has four minutes to build a tower as high as they can get it. They may stack the cups any way they wish, but not inside each other. The only other rule is that everyone on the team must help build the tower. If the tower falls down, they may start over.

 tip If the children don't catch on to making a base of inverted cups on which to build a tower, you may want to suggest they try that.

After four minutes, take a look at the towers and find something nice to say about each one (Creative! Cool design! Solidly built! Uses lots of cups!). Have the older children help you use the tape to measure how tall the tallest tower is. Ask the children if they think their towers would stand better on something soft and squishy like sand or a thick carpet, or on something hard, like a tabletop or bare floor. Agree with them that when we're building something, we need to put it on a good, solid foundation. Remind them (if they don't mention it themselves) that in today's Bible story, that's exactly what two different builders found out.

tip A fun alternative to the cups, especially with second and third graders, is gumdrops and pretzel sticks. Let kids use these materials to build their high towers—and encourage them to eat the building materials when the contest is over! When you see that most groups are finished or nearly so, review the structures, finding something positive to say about each one. Bridge to today's parable of the wise and foolish builders.

2 KNOW

Today's Parable Retold

Goal
Tell what happened to both houses when the storm came.

Time
10 minutes

Materials
☐ Plastic tablecloth (solid color is best)
☐ Large flat rock
☐ Sand in baggie
☐ Bag of blocks or wood pieces for building the house on sand
☐ House assembled (prior to your session) from Lego or Duplo plastic blocks
☐ Bible
☐ All the above placed in a toolbox
☐ Watering can filled with water

Spread out the plastic tablecloth and have the children help you retell the story they heard in your large group session. (If the children did not see the drama, ask them to listen to the story of the parable of the wise and foolish builders. Show them where the story is found in your Bible. Explain that this is another parable that Jesus told to help people listen to him and obey him.)

The story follows:

Once there was a very wise man who decided to build a house. "I think I'll build my house on a very strong foundation," he said to himself. "I'll build it on this nice, hard rock." (**Take rock out and ask child to place it somewhere as the house's foundation.**) Then the wise man built his house right on top of that rock. (**Have a child place the preassembled plastic block house on the rock.**)

Not long afterward, the wind started to blow against the little house. (**Have kids cup their mouths and make blowing sound.**) And the rain poured down on the little house. (**Have a child pour some water from the watering can onto the house.**) The rivers and streams around the house began to rise, and the streets were filled with water. It was a very bad storm. But what do you think happened to the house that the wise man built? Do you think it fell down? (**Pause for response.**) No way!

Then along came a foolish man who also decided to build a house. "I think I'll build my house on this nice sand," he said to himself. "It really doesn't matter if sand isn't very strong. It never storms much here anyway." (**Take bag of sand from toolbox and hand it to child to arrange as a foundation for the house.**) Then the foolish man built his house right on top of the sand. (**Quickly build a simple and unstable house from blocks or pieces of wood.**)

Not long afterward, the wind started to blow against the little house. (**Have kids cup their mouths and make blowing sound.**) And the rain poured down on the little house. (**Have a child pour some water from the watering can onto the house.**) The rivers and streams around the house began to rise, and the streets were filled with water. It was a very bad storm. What do you think happened to the house that the foolish man built? Do you think it fell down? (**Pause for response.**) Yes, that's exactly what happened! The house fell down with a huge crash! (**Have a child knock down the little house, while the others make crashing noises.**)

After Jesus told this story, he explained what it meant. "If you listen to me and do what I say, then you are like the wise man who built his house on the rock. But if you listen to me and don't do what I say, then you are like the foolish man who built his house on the sand."

You may want to listen to or sing one of today's songs to conclude your storytelling time.

Option to step 2

Storybook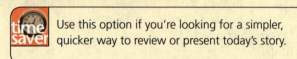

Time
5-10 minutes

Materials
☐ Storybook, "The Wise and Foolish Builders" (reproducible pages 191-192), copied and assembled

Assemble a sample storybook before class and show the children the pictures as you read through the pages together. You may want to ask an older child to read the story to the others. If so, try to get a copy of the book to the child before today's session so that he or she can practice reading it at home.

> **time saver** — Use this option if you're looking for a simpler, quicker way to review or present today's story.

Another possibility is to just look at the pictures in the book together and have the children tell as many of the details of the story as they can remember from the drama in the large group session.

If your photocopy machine has an enlarging feature, you may want to enlarge the pages of the storybook to full size, making it easier for the children to see the book as you read it. Or, if you're artistic, copy the simple drawings and text yourself onto full-size pages.

3 GROW
Listen and Do

Goal
Ask Jesus to help us listen and obey.

Time
10 minutes

Materials
None needed

Summarize the parable once more: **Jesus wants us to *listen* to what he says and then *do* it!** Have the group repeat "Listen and Do!" a time or two. Ask them if they can think of some good motions to go with that phrase that will help everyone remember it (for example, a hand cupped behind the ear for *listen*; fingers wiggling, hands moving for *do*). Repeat, using the motions they suggested.

Ask everyone to stand up. Say something like this: **I'm going to say some things that I want you to listen very carefully to. If you think I'm saying something Jesus would want us to do, stand straight and tall, just like the house on the rock. If you think I'm saying something Jesus would *not* want us to do, fall down on the floor, just like the house built on the sand. Stay on the floor until you hear something Jesus would want us to do. Then get up and stand up straight again. Ready?**

Read these statements or invent your own:
- Jesus wants us to listen when someone reads God's Word.

- Jesus doesn't care if we do what God's Word says, as long as we listen to it.
- Jesus wants us to be like the person who built a house on the sand.
- Jesus says we are wise if we listen to God's Word and do it.
- Jesus wants us to build our lives on him by obeying him.
- Jesus wants us to always think of ourselves first, then others.
- Jesus wants us to pray only on Sunday.
- Jesus wants us to hurt others when they hurt us.
- Jesus wants us to be kind to others.
- Jesus wants us to tell the truth always.

tip: After a few statements, let the children take turns making statements of their own. Participate along with the rest of the group by standing or falling!

Listen and Do Prayer Litany Word Smart   Self Smart

Option to step 3

Time
10-15 minutes

Materials
☐ Newsprint, marker

Summarize the parable once more: Jesus wants us to *listen* to what he says, then *do* it. Then work together with your children to compose a "listen and do" prayer litany. Explain that a litany usually has a chorus or refrain said by the entire group after the leader says a line. Your group response could be something like "Help us, Lord, to listen to you and do what you say" or simply "Help us listen and do" or "We will listen and do." Write the group response that the children decide to use on your newsprint, leaving space above it for the first line in your litany.

Next ask each child to think of something that Jesus wants us to do (give an example or two from the regular step). Be ready to help younger children, as necessary.

On your newsprint write each child's statement as they dictate it to you; for example, "Jesus wants us to tell the truth." Put the first statement just above your chosen refrain. Then ask another child to give you his or her idea of what Jesus wants us to do. Follow it with a star or asterisk that stands for the repeated refrain so that you don't have to print it over and over.

tip: If you have lots of beginning readers in your group, ask an older child who reads well to read the individual statements of the children. All the children can recite the refrain in unison.

When each child has contributed a statement, read your litany together. Have each child read his or her statement aloud, followed by the group response said in unison.

Point to the statements as they are read so that the children can follow along and keep their place. End your litany with **Amen**.

If the children enjoyed this activity, you could have them repeat their litany as part of your next large group gathering.

4 SHOW
Unit and Session Projects

Goal
Remind ourselves and others to listen and obey.
Time
15-30 minutes or more
Materials
See individual projects for lists

Below are a variety of projects to help the children apply this parable to their lives. Some of the projects are continuations from the first session and can run for the entire unit, others are for just this week. Choose one or more that best suits your time frame and the interests/abilities of the children.

Unit Project Ideas

Memory Fun Word Smart   Body Smart

Time
5-10
Materials
☐ Memory Fun (reproducible page 181)
☐ Bible
☐ Flashlight

Comment that today the children heard another wonderful story that Jesus told, another story from God's Word (hold up your Bible). Ask if anyone remembers the verse you started learning together last week from the Bible (show the children the reproducible page you sent home with them). If no one remembers, take out your flashlight and turn it on. Tell the children that the verse was about light and it begins with, "Your word is . . ."

It's very possible that none of the children will know the verse yet. If some do, have them recite it for the group. Otherwise, say the verse slowly while holding the flashlight. Repeat it, and then ask the children to say it once together. If you have time, pass the flashlight from child to child and ask each child to repeat as much as he or she can remember of the verse, then pass the light to the next child. Go around the circle, giving each child a chance. Praise the children for their good memories and ask them to continue learning the verse at home!

Sharable Parable Bookmarks Picture Smart   Word Smart

Time
15-20
Materials
☐ Bookmark pattern (reproducible page 187)
☐ Crayons
☐ Paper punch
☐ Construction paper, various colors
☐ Glue sticks
☐ Small pieces of ribbon

If the children enjoyed this craft last time, have them repeat it for today's session, coloring or decorating their bookmarks with symbols that reflect today's story.

Run copies of the pattern (p. 187) on heavy stock. Younger children can simply color in the circles to make a picture or design that reminds them of today's parable. Older children can glue on paper-punched circles of various colors of construction paper for a mosaic look.

For today's session, an outline of a house, a picture of a rock, or perhaps the words "Listen and do" would make an appropriate design. Notice that there's room at the bottom of the bookmark to print a title or the Scripture location of the parable. Attach a ribbon through a hole punched at the top of the bookmark.

Encourage kids to show the bookmark to their families and friends and to share the parable with them.

Storybooks Word Smart Picture Smart People Smart

Time
15 minutes
Materials
☐ Storybook, "The Wise and Foolish Builders" (reproducible pages 191-192), one set per child
☐ Crayons or markers

To make today's storybook, photocopy pages 191-192 and distribute a set to each child. Walk the children through the folding process, offering your help and the help of older children to the little ones in your group.

1. Fold both pages in half horizontally along the dotted lines.

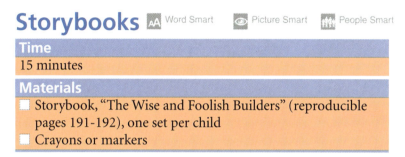

2. Fold both pages in half vertically along the dotted lines.

3. Insert the second set of folded pages into the first set, so that page 3 is opposite page 2.

Have kids print their names on the cover, then color in the pictures. (If short on time, just read the booklet with them and let them color it at home.) Encourage them to read the story with their family and friends.

One-Session Project Ideas
Paper House and Builder

Earth Smart   Picture Smart   Body Smart

Time
20-30 minutes

Materials
☐ House pattern (reproducible page 193), copied on heavy white paper, one per child
☐ Roof pattern (reproducible page 194), copied on heavy white paper, one per child
☐ Builder pattern (reproducible page 195), copied on heavy white paper, one per child
☐ Scissors
☐ Glue or tape
☐ Crayons, colored pencils, markers
☐ Container of sand (one per classroom)
☐ Large flat rock

time saver — If you're teaching young children, you can save a lot of time (and maybe some tears!) by cutting the patterns out for the children ahead of the session.

Making their own house is a fun way for the children to remind themselves to listen and do. They can also use the finished house to share the parable with someone else.

Walk the children through the following steps, letting them all complete a step before moving on. Having a helper or two around will make things a lot easier if you're teaching young children or if you have a large group.

1. Use crayons and markers to color and decorate the triangles of the roof and the four walls of the house.

2. Cut out the roof and house along all outer edges, including the tabs.

3. Fold all four triangles of roof up, then fold all of the tabs toward the inside of each triangle.

4. Fold all four walls of the house down, then fold all of the tabs toward the inside of each wall.

5. Put a small amount of glue on each tab, then glue the tabs to the inside of the roof triangles and the house walls. You can strengthen the structure by also taping on the outside, if you wish.

6. Glue the roof to the house.

7. Color and cut out the builder and the stand. Cut the four slits; fold the stand on the dotted lines. Insert the builder's slits into the slits of the stand.

Set up an area of the room with a container of sand and a large flat rock. The children can use the props to tell the story to each other, using their house and builder.

 tip — Tell kids they should merely tip the house over, not destroy it, when telling about the foolish builder. Sounds obvious, but if you don't, someone will smash her house faster than you can say, "Don't do that!"

Clappers Body Smart   Music Smart

Time
20-25 minutes
Materials
☐ Wooden paint stir sticks, two per child
☐ Cardboard scraps (thick, corrugated)
☐ Red duct tape (available at hardware and craft stores)
☐ Craft glue
☐ Felt strips in various bright colors
☐ Sharp scissors for kids (Fiskars work well)

Show your sample craft as you explain that a clapper is a percussion instrument of a style and design that has been used for thousands of years in many different countries. Demonstrate how to use the clapper by slapping it gently against your palm; point out how the decorative felt serves as padding for the player's hand. Clappers sound great as a rhythm instrument during singing time and during the summer celebration program.

Prior to your session, cut cardboard scraps into 1" x 2" (2.5 x 5 cm) pieces, one per child. During your session, walk kids through these steps as they make their own clappers:

1. Fold the cardboard piece in half and place it between two stir sticks where there is a curve in the wood. The creased end of the cardboard piece should be facing down toward the bottom of the handle, like this:

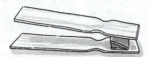

2. Glue the sides of the cardboard to the stir sticks.
3. Tightly wrap two or three 5" (12.5 cm) pieces of red duct tape around the bottom of the clapper. This will create a handle for the instrument that is approximately 4" (10 cm) long when completed.

 To save time, you and your helpers can complete steps 1-3 prior to your session.. This will also simplify the construction process for younger children.

4. From the felt strips, cut out small, narrow houses, water, rocks, sand, rain drops, and clouds. Glue them to the clapper.
   Your finished clapper will look something like this:

Be sure to take time to show the children how to gently strike the clapper against their palms. Practice using the clapper with one of the songs for today's session (see large groups session, CD tracks 3-5).

Nuts and Bolts Trail Mix

Time
5-10 minutes
Materials
☐ Small sealable bags filled with Cheerios, pretzel sticks or twists, Chex, or any other food that bears some resemblance to building materials
☐ "Tool stickers" to decorate bags (optional)
☐ Cold drink, cups

OK, so you may have to tell the kids that the contents of the baggies is supposed to resemble tools. They won't mind. Serve the goodies while the children work on one of the projects for this step.

Storybook: *Parables Jesus Told*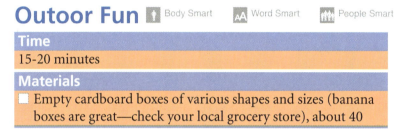

Time
10 minutes
Materials
☐ *Parables Jesus Told,* Tell-Me Stories, Vol. 1, written by Ella K. Lindvall; illustrated by H. Kent Puckett (Moody Press)

Your group will enjoy hearing "Two Men and Their Houses," one of the parables told in this book. They'll also enjoy looking at the pictures, which are simple, yet bold and dramatic.

Outoor Fun Body Smart   Word Smart   People Smart

Time
15-20 minutes
Materials
☐ Empty cardboard boxes of various shapes and sizes (banana boxes are great—check your local grocery store), about 40

Here's a bigger, outdoor version of the construction game you may have used to begin today's session. Go outside and divide kids into two groups. Tell the groups their task is to build a house—one group builds the house on the rock, the other the house on the sand. Give the groups their assignment and tell them they have five minutes to assemble their houses from the boxes you supply. The only rule is that everyone must help.

After five minutes call time and see what the kids have produced. Find something good to say about each house. Then have the two groups tell the story about their house. It would be cool to have your entire church school or VBS witness the story telling.

Small Group Session: Grades 4-8

The Parable of the Wise and Foolish Builders

Scripture
Matthew 7:24-27

Memory Challenge
Matthew 7:24-27

Focus
Jesus teaches us to build our lives on him by obeying him.

Goal
Introduce the parable of the wise and foolish builders.
Time
10 minutes
Materials
☐ Notecards, several packets ☐ Scissors ☐ Tape measure ☐ Tape ☐ Trail-mix snack (see below) and cold drink (optional)

Here's a building game older kids will enjoy. Divide into groups of two or three; give each group the same number of cards (at least forty or fifty to start with). Place additional cards in a "lumberyard" for groups that run out of cards and need more to continue building.

Explain that each team has four minutes to make as high a tower as they can with the cards. If they wish, they may use the scissors and tape. Cards can be taped, cut, rolled, and stacked in any way. The structures must stand on their own, without support from any team member. Team members may start over if their towers collapse. They may not knock down each other's structures.

 tip In the unlikely event that team members are puzzled as to how to build their towers, you could show them just one trick: cutting a half-inch slit in the top left and right of each card, and then inserting other cards into those slits. But let them discover this and other techniques for themselves, if at all possible.

After four minutes, see which tower is the highest (use tape measure if it's a close call) but find something good to say about each tower (Creative! Sturdy! Cool design!). If you wish, reward your construction engineers with "nuts and bolts" trail mix (see recipe at end of this session). Serve with a cold drink.

What's This For? 🚶 Body Smart ❖ Number Smart

Option to step 1

Time
5 minutes
Materials
☐ Building bits and pieces that have no apparent function: a strange kind of nut and bolt, funny-looking pliers, a basin wrench, car parts, motor parts, and so on

Try this if your group has older kids who are interested in tools, cars, and construction. It's an idea shamelessly borrowed from the TV show *This Old House,* during which the producers of the show take turns inventing possible uses for odd-looking tools, machine parts, and so on. The idea is not to guess correctly but to come up with creative uses that sound convincing.

Scrounge around your garage or basement, collect some strange-looking stuff, and give one item to each group of two to four kids. Tell them their task is to invent a use for this . . . whatever it is.

Enjoy the show. Then bridge to the construction tools used by the builders in our story for today—like the sand pail and shovel used by the Sandyland builders in our large group skit.

② KNOW 🚶 Body Smart 👪 People Smart AA Word Smart
Getting into the Parable

Goal
Retell the parable of the two builders.
Time
10 minutes
Materials
☐ Bibles
☐ "The Wise and Foolish Builders" (pp. 137-140)

If you didn't have a large group session, your kids will enjoy presenting the skit on pages 137-140 of this leader's guide. You needn't supply all the costumes and props suggested for the large group presentation, unless of course you happen to have some hard hats, hammers, saws, pails, and so on to bring. If not, just have group members take the various parts (seven speaking roles) and read the skit. See the large group presentation for more ideas.

If your group has already seen the dramatization, you can quickly review it with a fun skit similar to that suggested for session 1. The parable of the wise and foolish builders is perfect for a variety of fun roles (rain, wind, houses) and actions (wind blowing against the house, house crashing down).

Ask for volunteers to portray the following:
- the house built on the rock (two or more kids)
- the house built on the sand (two or more kids)
- the rain (any number of kids)
- the stream (any number of kids)
- the wind (any number of kids)
- the wise builder
- the foolish builder
- the rock (one or two kids), optional
- the sand (one or two kids), optional

 tip If you're thinking this little drama requires a huge group of kids, don't worry. Just assign kids to multiple roles.

Begin by opening your Bible to Matthew 7:24-27 and reading **"Everyone who hears these words of mine and puts them into practice is like a wise man who built his house on the rock."** *(Kid playing wise builder pretends to build a house using two or more kids who stand with their arms together in the shape of a house; if kids are playing the rock, have them lie on the floor at the feet of the kids who are pretending to be the house.)*

Continue: **"The rain came down . . ."** *(Kids playing rain make descending motions with arms and bodies.)*

"The streams rose . . ." *(Kids playing stream make ascending motions with arms and bodies.)*

"The wind blew and beat against that house; yet it did not fall. *(Kids playing wind making blowing noises and push at the house; house sways but stays upright.)*

And so on, until you finish the parable at verse 27. If you wish, continue reading the next two verses without having them acted out.

Then distribute Bibles and ask, **If you were to put the meaning of this parable into a short phrase or slogan, what would you say?** Direct kids back to verses 23 and 26 as they think about this. Then agree on a statement or two that the whole group can accept, perhaps something like "Listen to Jesus; do what he says."

Option to step 2

Same Story, Different Versions 🆎 Word Smart

Time
10 minutes
Materials
☐ "Same Story, Different Versions" (reproducible page 197), one copy per person
☐ Copy of each Bible quoted on the reproducible sheet (optional)

Use this option if you'd rather not do another skit in the fashion described above and if you'd like your group to get a sense of the range of translations and paraphrases that are available. This activity will be especially meaningful if your students are memorizing this parable.

Distribute copies of "Same Story, Different Versions" and ask for volunteers to read the parable as told by different Bible translators. Then ask questions like these:

 If kids liked a particular version, encourage them to use that version at home when reading the Bible.

- Compare the way the different versions state the message of the parable. How would you state that message in a simple sentence or a slogan?
- What are some differences between the versions?
- Which version or versions do you prefer? Why?

3 GROW

Self Smart
Word Smart

Survey: Where Am I in This Parable?

Goal
Reflect on where we are in this parable.
Time
10 minutes
Materials
☐ "Where Am I in This Parable?" (reproducible page 199), one copy per person
☐ Pen or pencil

After the lively time of acting out the story (previous step), this activity will provide a quiet, personal time of reacting to the story. Distribute a copy of "Where Am I in This Parable?" to each person. Ask them to complete the multiple choice items and the items calling for a written response. Explain that their responses will be private unless they choose to share.

Allow five minutes for filling out the sheets, then take a moment to talk about some ways we see and hear Jesus in our lives (item 2). Which of these ways (or other ways) does the group think are most useful for them at this point in their lives?

You might want to share your own response to item 4 so that kids will know that at one time or another, all of us become "foolish builders" who know very well what God wants us to do but fail to do it. The big thing is not that we are perfect but that we have built our lives on Jesus, whom we trust and who loves us dearly.

You may want to discuss item 5 ("One thing that helps me do what I know is right") with the entire group.

If you are working with middle school kids, also challenge them to reflect on what "flood" might look like in their lives. When everything is going fine in their life, it may not seem to make much difference if they follow Jesus' teaching. But once the floods hit, it makes all the difference in the world. Ask kids to name some of the crisis times that sooner or later hit all of us (illness, accident, death of loved ones, and so on).

Conclude this step by having a time of silent prayer, during which each person may actually say to Jesus whatever he or she wrote for the last item on the survey.

 tip If some of your students prefer drawing to writing, let them make a sketch or collage instead of taking the survey. They could show themselves as part of the parable or they could picture the way(s) they could respond to it.

4 SHOW
Unit and Session Projects

Goal
Remind ourselves and others to listen and obey.
Time
15-30 minutes or more
Materials
See individual projects for lists

Below are a variety of projects to help group members apply this parable to their lives. Some of the projects are continuations from the first session and can run for the entire unit, others are for just this session. Choose one or more that best suits your time frame and the interests/abilities of the children.

Unit Project Ideas

Memorize and Share a Parable  Word Smart

Time
5 minutes
Materials
☐ Bibles
☐ Memory Challenge (reproducible page 183 or 184)
☐ Pencils

Tell the group that you have a challenge for them—a Memory Challenge. Beginning this week and for the rest of the unit, you'd like them to work on memorizing the parable they heard today: the wise and foolish builders. Read through the whole passage again from the Bible. Then give each student a copy of the Memory Challenge and challenge them to memorize as much of the first two verses (vv. 24-25) of this passage as they can before your next session.

Sharable Parable Bookmarks Picture Smart Word Smart

Time
5-10 minutes
Materials
☐ Bookmark pattern (reproducible page 187)
☐ Markers
☐ Paper punch
☐ Construction paper, various colors
☐ Paper punch
☐ Glue sticks
☐ Small pieces of ribbon

If your group enjoyed this craft last time, have them repeat it for today's session, coloring or decorating their bookmarks with symbols that reflect today's story. Run copies of the pattern (see page 187) on heavy stock. Kids can color in the circles to make a design that connects to today's story or glue on paper-punched circles of various colors of construction paper for a mosaic look.

For today's session, an outline of a house or perhaps the words "Listen and do" would make an appropriate design. Notice that there's room at the bottom of the bookmark to print a title or the Scripture location of the parable. Attach a ribbon through a hole punched at the top of the bookmark.

Sun Art Picture Smart   Earth Smart

Time
15-20 minutes per session

Materials
☐ Construction paper in various dark colors
☐ Removable glue sticks (check your local craft store)
☐ Scissors
☐ Toothpicks
☐ Pen

This project, adapted from a Martha Stewart newspaper column, uses the power of the sun to make a unique kind of art. Kids can make interesting illustrations related to the parables they're learning. The basic idea is to place cutout shapes on a sheet of colored construction paper. Cut out shapes from construction paper and glue with removable glue to the sheet. Then tape the sheet, cutouts facing out, to a window where it will catch a lot of sun. After a week or so (longer if higher contrast is desired), peel off the cutouts. Their images will be bold and sharp on the construction paper, while the paper surrounding the images has faded in color.

For today's session on the parable of the wise and foolish builders, kids could make cutouts of houses and builders to glue on their construction paper. Or they could use toothpicks to make a sharp outline of the houses and the builders. Letters can also be used as cutouts for those who want to label their artwork.

Kids can take this project home today, hang it in a sunny window, and let the sun do its work for a week or so. Encourage them to show their art to their family and/or friends and explain how it relates to the parable of the two builders.

One-Session Project Ideas

Clappers Body Smart   Music Smart

Time
20-25 minutes

Materials
☐ Wooden paint stir sticks, two per child
☐ Cardboard scraps (thick, corrugated)
☐ Red duct tape (available at hardware and craft stores)
☐ Craft glue
☐ Felt strips in various bright colors
☐ Scissors

Show your sample craft to the group as you explain that a clapper is a percussion instrument of a kind that has been used for thousands of years in many different countries. Demonstrate how to use the clapper by slapping it gently against your palm; point out how the decorative felt serves as padding for the player's hand.

Clappers sound great when played to the rhythm of songs. Or they could be used to accent the beat of a rap. Older kids may want to make some extra clappers to give to younger kids they know.

Prior to your session, cut cardboard scraps into 1" x 2" (2.5 x 5 cm) pieces, one per child. During your session, walk kids through these steps as they make their own clappers:

1. Fold the cardboard piece in half and place it between two stir sticks where there is a curve in the wood. The creased end of the cardboard piece should be facing down toward the bottom of the handle, like this:

2. Glue the sides of the cardboard to the stir sticks.

3. Tightly wrap two or three 5" (12.5 cm) pieces of red duct tape around the bottom of the clapper. This will create a handle for the instrument that is approximately 4" (10 cm) long when completed.

4. From the felt strips, cut out small, narrow houses, water, rocks, sand, rain drops, and clouds. Glue them to the two sides of the clapper.

Your finished clapper will look something like this:

Practice using the clapper with one of the songs for today's session (see large group session, CD tracks 3-5).

Writing a Story Rap   Word Smart   Music Smart

Time
20 minutes
Materials
☐ Clappers from previous step (optional) ☐ Newsprint ☐ Markers

Here's a fun follow-up to the previous activity of making clappers. Suggest that kids work in small groups to write a rap based on the parable of the wise and foolish builders. Encourage them to work in the message of the parable as well as its actions. They could put the message in a refrain if they wish. When finished, kids could use their clappers to accent the beat of their rap.

Chances are your kids will know more about rap and writing raps than you can tell them, but if you feel the need to, you can say that the lines usually rhyme and that the beat can vary a bit from line to line.

Here's a sample you can give them if they need a push to get going:

> *You wanna be WISE, you wanna be COOL?*
> *Then build on JE-sus, and don't be a FOOL.*

Give the groups plenty of time to finish their raps. Then have them present it to the rest of the class, using their clappers (or, if they didn't make the clappers, just clapping their hands or slapping their knees to the beat).

Nuts and Bolts Trail Mix   Body Smart

Time
5-10 minutes
Materials
☐ Sealable bags filled with Cheerios, pretzel sticks or twists, Chex, or any other food that bears some resemblance to building materials ☐ "Tool stickers" to decorate outside of sealable bags (optional) ☐ Cold drinks, cups

OK, so you may have to tell the kids that the contents of the baggies are supposed to resemble tools. They won't mind. Serve the goodies while they work on one of the projects for this step.

Outdoor Fun   Body Smart   Word Smart   People Smart

Time
15-20
Materials
☐ Empty cardboard boxes of various shapes and sizes (banana boxes are great—check your local grocery store), about 40

Here's a bigger, outdoor version of the construction game you may have used to begin today's session. Go outside and divide kids into two groups. Tell the groups their task is to build a house—one group builds the house on the rock, the other the house on the sand. Give the groups their assignment and tell them they have five minutes to assemble their houses from the boxes you supply. The only rule is that everyone must help.

After five minutes call time and see what the kids have produced. Find something good to say about each house. Then have the two groups tell the story about their house. It would be cool to have your entire church school or VBS witness the story telling.

Large Group Session

3 The Great Banquet

Scripture
Luke 14:15-24

Focus
Jesus teaches us that God invites all kinds of people to become part of his family (kingdom).

WORDSearch

Think About It

The Great Banquet, a parable about the kingdom of God, ends abruptly with a scathing indictment. If you know something about the folks to whom Jesus was telling this parable, you probably have already picked up on why Jesus gave that indictment. The context helps us out here. Jesus had gone to eat at the home of a prominent Pharisee. Naturally, many other Pharisees and experts in the law of God were also there, but all eyes were on Jesus. Checking him out. Testing him. They were suspicious of Jesus. He seemed, after all, to always have an answer for them. And when they got home and thought about his answers, they realized that often his teaching was a slap in their faces.

The Pharisees and teachers of the law were the best and the brightest that Israel had to offer. They were God's lawkeepers—to the letter. They even legislated and kept their *own* laws to help them keep *God's* laws. By keeping these laws so carefully, they thought they had put themselves on a regimented, work-hard path to God. They were working their way up, and they knew it. They were Jews, God's chosen people. A proud, exclusive club. No sinners, no outsiders (non-Jews) allowed.

Jesus is working the room before the meal, talking with whoever wants to listen. At last, the dinner bell rings. The host, of course, is seated at the head of the table, but no one else has a reserved seat, so a polite free-for-all ensues. Who can grab the seat of honor? Everyone's been keeping one eye on Jesus and one eye on that special seat near the host. The bell rings and the race is on. Until Jesus clears his throat and says, "False start. Back to the starting line!" With all eyes on him, Jesus explains, "Look, don't go around thinking you're better than everybody else. Imagine your embarrassment if you sat down at a seat of honor, and the host made you move! Take a less honorable seat—who knows, maybe you'll even get promoted." It's a common-sense teaching of course, one they all should have known and lived by, but then Jesus adds this zinger: "In fact, when you throw a banquet, don't invite all your chummy friends. Instead, invite those who could never possibly throw you a banquet back." Now this was new! I'm sure more than a few of them were scratching their heads.

But one of the guests seems to catch on. He senses that Jesus has a deeper meaning in mind here. And so he wisely says,

> **Pray About It**
> Pray that Jesus' words in this parable will help you see how diverse God's kingdom is. Pray that you will come to appreciate that other believers may look or talk or act a whole lot different than you, but they are still believers in Jesus Christ. Pray that you will never underestimate the generosity of God's grace that showers down upon so many diverse groups of people. Pray that you will never position yourself or your family or your congregation or your community at the place of honor at the table as if, like a Pharisee, you earned it by virtue of who you are—for none of us is worthy. Pray that you will see that one thing unites us all: we are all sinners who need a Savior.

> **Tell About It**
> Tell the children that God invites many different kinds of people into his kingdom. Tell them that all those in the kingdom of God—all so different—are also so much the same. We all need a Savior. God gave Jesus to us to save us. Above all, tell the children to accept the invitation of Jesus into the kingdom of God.

"Blessed is the man who will eat at the feast in the kingdom of God." Can you picture everyone? They're all raising their index fingers and simultaneously saying: "Ahhhhhh! Sheer brilliance."

Jesus, of course, just smiles as he is ushered into yet another teachable moment by these folks who know so much. And Jesus tells them the parable of the great banquet. They really couldn't miss the point of his story: "You people who think you're chosen, who think you have it all coming, who think you're working your way up to God, you are failing to do one very important thing. You're not accepting the invitation of the King. You're assuming that you're going to the banquet. You're trying to barge in. But you haven't said yes. You haven't said thanks. Don't you know your invitation is about to expire? There's not much time left. And when it's too late, it's too late. You won't even be able to snatch a mint or a peanut off the guest book table. You'll be left out of the banquet hall."

What an indictment of the very people sitting all around Jesus! Talk about a parable of judgment.

But for those who, unlike the Pharisees and teachers of the law, believed in Jesus, there's a happy ending. The Master says, "Go out of town and bring people back. I don't care what they look like. I don't care if they're poor or blind or lame. I want them regardless. I want them to say yes and I want them to say thank you. I want them to come. Keep searching them out, no matter who they are, until this house of mine is filled up."

So there you have it—a parable of judgment that ends with incredible mercy, with God's indiscriminate grace. Those who believe they deserve a place at God's banquet based on their own goodness are not welcome. But all those who rely on Jesus definitely are welcome. God wants his banquet hall filled with all kinds of people. Isaiah (ch. 60) foretells it. He describes the New Jerusalem being filled to the brim with the nations, with the wealth of the nations, with the culture of the nations, with the kings of the nations, with the people of the nations. The people come from all over—through deserts, across the seas, all bringing all their gifts to the king. They come from every nation. Think of all those languages! It's like Babel reversed. It's like Pentecost turbocharged. It's like the new creation as it will be. And it's because the Lamb, Jesus, was slain and "with [his] blood . . . purchased men for God from every tribe and language and people and nation" (Rev. 5:9). All of us at a great banquet together—some looking like us, many looking unlike us, but all of them looking like neighbors, like those who have said yes to Jesus' invitation.

Can you imagine it?

Planning the Session

The parable of the great banquet offers a wonderful opportunity to emphasize the diversity of God's family, the church, and to issue an invitation to become a part of that family. Watch for times in your group session when you can mention and model these truths.

If you're planning on presenting the celebration program, you may want to budget some extra time for singing so that kids can review the songs from the last session and learn the new ones for this session.

The suggestions in this large group session assume that you'll be dramatizing the parable of the two builders to children and young teens and preparing them to respond to it in small groups.

Singing

As kids enter, play the song "Ha La La La" from the CD (track 1). Invite the kids to join you in singing this fun action song. You may also want to review "Stop and Let Me Tell You" (track 2) and "He Is the Rock" (track 5). All three songs are suggested as part of the summer celebration program.

Two new songs are suggested for today's session. The first is "Big House" (track 7), a song with a strong beat and lots of actions that especially younger kids will enjoy. (It's also suggested for the summer celebration program.) "The Great Parade" (track 8) joyfully expresses the great diversity of people in God's kingdom.

Drama

Before presenting "The Great Banquet" ask someone—preferably a good reader from your middle school—to read the parable from Luke 14:15-24, using an easy-to-understand version such as the NIrV or New Living Bible.

For today's drama you'll need the script on pages 141-143 and six readers. Please see session 1 for general comments regarding drama teams, memorizing lines, and presenting the drama without rehearsal.

> **tip**
> You can easily add nonspeaking roles to the drama by having younger children be on stage as "people on the street" when Seriah is searching the countryside for people to invite to the banquet. As Seriah approaches, they can pretend to listen, then reject the unspoken invitation with a wave of the hand or by shaking their head.

For today's set you'll need a table in the background, set for dinner, to suggest the banquet hall. Or you can leave the stage empty, with the audience simply assuming the banquet table is offstage, perhaps through a set of exit doors. You'll also need stage space for the encounters between Seriah and those who are invited to the banquet. Please see the drama for details.

Characters can be dressed in contemporary everyday clothes or in first-century garb (bathrobes, sandals, head covering), whatever you prefer. A few simple props—clipboards, a map, a large pail, a box of chocolates or bunch of flowers—are all that's required. Seriah may carry a Palm Pilot if she's in the contemporary mode. See page 141 for details.

The skit features reporter/narrator Rehoboam, who acts like a "fly on the wall," watching the action and occasionally breaking into the story to offer comment. This is a key role in the skit. The roles of Seriah and Orpah were written with female readers in mind; however, you should feel free to change the gender (and names) of any of the characters. Just insert your changes into the script before photocopying it.

Small Groups

After the drama, children will again meet in small groups. Notice that we've included two session plans—one for children in kindergarten-grade 3 and another for children in grades 4-8. If your regular church school leaders are present, it's probably best to have the children meet in their groups as usual; however, you could also choose to combine several groups together. Each small group leader will need to adapt the plan to the needs of his or her children.

Small Group Session: Kindergarten-Grade 3

3 The Great Banquet

Scripture
Luke 14:15-24

Memory Fun
Psalm 119:105

Focus
Jesus teaches us that God invites all kinds of people to become part of his family (kingdom).

1 HELLO — You're Invited!

Body Smart
Word Smart

Goal
Enjoy a snack and prepare for the Bible story.

Time
10 minutes

Materials
☐ Snack, cold drink, cups
☐ Napkins
☐ Picnic blanket
☐ Picnic basket (optional)
☐ Balloons of various shapes and colors, crepe paper (optional)

As each child enters the room, say, "[Name], you're invited to a picnic!" Weather permitting, take the kids outdoors, spread your picnic blanket, and take the snack and drinks out of your basket. If the weather isn't cooperative, have your picnic in your room (which you may want to have the kids decorate with balloons and crepe paper).

While you're enjoying the snack together, ask some informal questions like these:

- Do you like parties and picnics? Why or why not?
- What are some reasons we have parties and picnics?
- How would you feel if you sent out invitations to your birthday party and everybody said, "Sorry. I can't come. I've got other things to do?"

tip: Serving cake as the snack will allow you to explain that at banquets, cake is often served for dessert.

Explain that today's Bible story is about very big party called a banquet. At a banquet all kinds of good foods are served. Jesus is the one who tells the story of this particular banquet.

62

2 KNOW
Today's Parable Retold

Word Smart
Body Smart

Goal
Tell what happened in Jesus' story about the banquet.

Time
10 minutes

Materials
☐ Bible
☐ Notecards with invitation written on one side, an excuse on the other (see below)

Before your meeting, prepare large notecards with a simple invitation on one side ("You are invited to my banquet. Please come!") and an excuse on the other. Print a different excuse on each card. The excuses should include the three given in the parable as well as additional ones you've made up. Here are a few suggestions:

- I cannot come. I just bought some land and I want go look it over.
- I cannot come. I just bought five teams of oxen and I need to check them out.
- I cannot come. I just got married and need to get home to my wife.
- I cannot come. I don't like banquets.
- I cannot come. I'm going to another party.
- I cannot come. Banquets give me a stomachache.
- I cannot come. I'm having my hair done.
- I cannot come. I don't have any fancy clothes to wear.
- I cannot come. I'm on a diet.
- I cannot come. I have company coming.
- I cannot come. I want to play with my friends.

If the children already saw the drama in your large group session, then use this time to retell and review the story, using the suggestions below.

Begin by showing the children where the story is found in the Bible (Luke 14:15-24). Then tell the story from the point of view of the person giving the banquet.

> **tip:** If you did not have a large group session, you may want to briefly tell or read the story to the children before you invite them to become involved in your first-person telling, as described in this step.

As you tell the story, choose a "helper" from the group who can hand out invitations to your banquet, one to each child. The helper may read the invitation as he or she hands them out: "You are invited to my banquet. Please come!" When the helper is finished, have him or her sit down with the rest of the group.

Pretend to be checking the preparations for the banquet. **Let's see—is the food all cooked just the way I ordered? Yes, I see it is. Are my very best dishes and glasses on the table, all carefully placed? Yes, I see they are.** Announce that your banquet is ready at last for all the guests to come and enjoy.

> **tip:** Have your cards arranged with the longest excuses on top. Whisper to your helper to give the top three cards to the older children who will be able to read them.

Pick a different helper (a stronger reader) and ask him or her to go to each child and ask if they can come to the banquet. Each child then reads the excuse on the backside of the card he or she is holding. If they wish, they can "act out" their reaction by shaking their head, waving the helper away, stomping a foot, and so on.

If some of the younger children are unable to read the excuses, have your helper say, "If you want some help reading your excuse, just hand me your card." The helper can then whisper the excuse to the child to say out loud.

After you've heard all the excuses, let the children see your reaction. **I am *so* disappointed and angry! Why won't anyone come to my banquet? They all have excuses, it seems!** Then brighten up as you say, **I have an idea! I'm going to invite *everybody* to my banquet. I don't care who they are or what they look like or how old or young they are. Everybody may come!**

Choose a third helper (a younger child) to go to all the kids and invite them to come to the party. This time everyone should follow your helper to the banquet. When they "arrive" have them sit down on the floor or around a table.

Say, **I see there is still room at my banquet table. I'm going to send my servant out once more to ask even more people to come to my banquet. I will ask *everyone* to come. I want my banquet hall full. Then I will be happy. But all those who said no, who refused to come, all those people will never get a taste of my banquet.**

Option to step 2

Storybook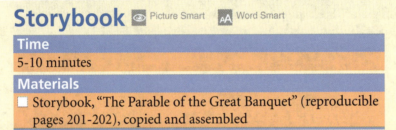

Time
5-10 minutes

Materials
☐ Storybook, "The Parable of the Great Banquet" (reproducible pages 201-202), copied and assembled

Assemble a sample storybook before class and show the children the pictures as you read through the pages together, or have the children retell the story by looking at the pictures. Another option is to ask an older child to read the story to the others. If so, try to get a copy of the book to the child before today's session so that he or she can practice reading it at home.

 Use this option if you're looking for a simpler, quicker way to review or present today's story.

If you have access to a photocopier with enlargement features, you could enlarge the pages of the storybook to full size, making it easier for the children to see the book as you read it. Or, if you're artistic, copy the simple drawings and text yourself onto full-size pages.

③ GROW
Join the Parade!

Goal
Feel happy that God invites many kinds of people to be part of his family.

Time
10 minutes

Materials
☐ People poster from session 1
☐ Song: "The Great Parade" (p. 165; CD, track 8)
☐ CD player
☐ Balloons of various sizes and colors
☐ Markers

If you made (and saved) the "people poster" in session 1 (Grow step), plan to use it again in this step. It will make a great illustration of the diversity of people in God's family.

Start by asking some questions about today's story, along these lines:
- **If you were invited to the banquet, would you have come?**
- **Why do you think people said no to the invitation?**
- **How many people did the man in Jesus' story want to come to his banquet?**
- **At the end of the story, what kind of people came to the banquet?** (According to the story, people who were poor, blind, lame, and so on. Expand that by asking kids if they think that *all kinds* of people came to the banquet.)
- **Do you think God wants a few or many people in his family?**
- **What kind of people do you think God wants his in family?** (All kinds!)

After this last question, display your poster and ask kids to describe some of the differences they see between the people on the poster: old, young, little, big, brown, tan, golden, white, smiling, sad,

If you didn't do the people poster in session 1 you might consider doing it now. See step 3 of session 1 for details.

and so on. Remind them that God wants all different kinds of people in his family—"people of all times and places and nations and races" as the text of the song "The Great Parade" describes.

Hand out balloons of various colors and sizes. Ask kids to imagine that the balloons—with their different colors and shapes—are like the many different people who are part of God's family. If time permits, have the children use markers to draw faces on the balloons; older children may write the names of different countries on the balloons.

Conclude by having a "parade" through the church or outside. Kids can wave their balloons and march as you play "The Great Parade" (CD track 8). You may want to replay the refrain and have the children sing it as they march.

4 SHOW
Unit and Session Projects

Goal
Be grateful for the different kinds of people in God's family as we share this parable with others.

Time
15-30 minutes or more

Materials
See individual projects for lists

Below are a variety of projects to help the children apply this parable to their lives. Some of the projects are continuations from the first session and run for the entire unit, others are for just this session. Choose one or more that best suits your time frame and the interests and abilities of your children.

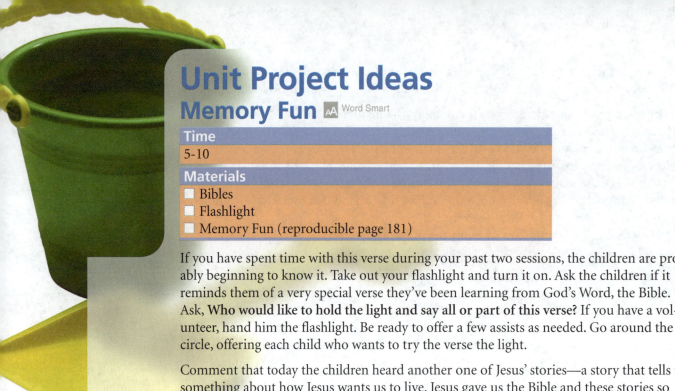

Unit Project Ideas

Memory Fun Word Smart

Time
5-10
Materials
☐ Bibles
☐ Flashlight
☐ Memory Fun (reproducible page 181)

If you have spent time with this verse during your past two sessions, the children are probably beginning to know it. Take out your flashlight and turn it on. Ask the children if it reminds them of a very special verse they've been learning from God's Word, the Bible. Ask, **Who would like to hold the light and say all or part of this verse?** If you have a volunteer, hand him the flashlight. Be ready to offer a few assists as needed. Go around the circle, offering each child who wants to try the verse the light.

Comment that today the children heard another one of Jesus' stories—a story that tells us something about how Jesus wants us to live. Jesus gave us the Bible and these stories so that we would know how to live as his children. That's what this Memory Fun tells us. The stories of Jesus are like a flashlight in a dark room. They help us see!

Sharable Parable Bookmarks Picture Smart   Word Smart

Time
15-20 minutes
Materials
☐ Bookmark pattern (reproducible page 187)
☐ Crayons
☐ Paper punch
☐ Construction paper, various colors
☐ Glue sticks
☐ Small pieces of ribbon

If the children enjoyed this craft before, have them repeat it for today's session, coloring or decorating their bookmarks with symbols that reflect today's story. Run copies of the pattern (see p. 187) on heavy stock. Younger children can simply color in the circles to make a picture or design that reminds them of parable. Older children can glue on paper-punched circles of various colors of construction paper for a mosaic look.

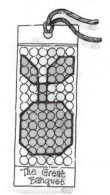

For today's session, a piece of fruit, a table, or a plate and glass would make an appropriate design. Notice that there's room at the bottom of the bookmark to print a title or the Scripture location of the parable. Attach a ribbon through a hole punched at the top of the bookmark.

Encourage kids to show the bookmark to their families and friends and to share the parable with them.

Storybooks Word Smart · Picture Smart · People Smart

Time
15 minutes
Materials
☐ Storybook, "The Parable of the Great Banquet" (reproducible pages 201-202), one set per child
☐ Crayons or markers

Each of the five sessions offers a take-home storybook that kids may share with their family and friends. For today's session, photocopy pages 201-202 and distribute a set to each child. Walk the children through the folding process, offering your help and the help of older children to the little ones in your group.

1. Fold both pages in half horizontally along the dotted lines.

2. Fold both pages in half vertically along the dotted lines.

3. Insert the second set of folded pages into the first set, so that page 3 is opposite page 2.

Have kids print their names on the cover, then color in the pictures. (If you're short on time, just read the booklet with them and let them color it at home.) Encourage them to read the story with their family and friends.

One-Session Project Ideas
Invitation Making

Body Smart · Number Smart · People Smart · Self Smart

Time
15-20 minutes
Materials
☐ Cardstock or light-colored construction paper
☐ Old magazines
☐ Scissors
☐ Glue sticks
☐ Bits of felt, ribbon, cut paper, and other materials to decorate cards
☐ Markers, colored pencils, crayons

Remind the children that God invites many different kinds of people to be part of his family. And God uses us to tell people about him so that they too can be part of God's family. We can invite neighbors, friends, and anyone else to come and learn about God.

Ask the children to think of someone they could invite to come to Sunday school with them, or to the summer celebration program, or to church, or just over to their house to play. They could also invite family members to gather and listen to a parable Jesus told (kids can use their take-home storybooks to share this week's story).

Wait until everyone has someone in mind (be ready to help out by making suggestions). Then ask the children to make an invitation to that person.

Distribute the cardstock or light-colored construction paper and the other materials you've brought for making invitations. Show them how to fold the cardstock in half (help younger children do this neatly). Some may want to cut people figures or lettering from magazines; others may prefer to draw their own illustrations or make a torn-paper collage.

Have the children show their invitations to each other when they're finished. Encourage them to give their invitations to the persons for whom they were made.

 If you're working with small children, you'll need volunteers who can print the words the children want to include on their invitations. Keep it simple!

Circle Game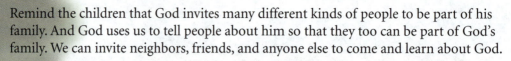

Time
10-15 minutes
Materials
☐ Two 15' (5 m) lengths of string, twine, or rope

This activity will help the children recognize some of the differences and similarities between them. You could also use the activity as an option to the Hello step, if you wish.

Move the chairs and tables to one side. Knot the ends of the strings into two loops and position on the floor as shown:

Gather children around the outside of the two rope circles and say that you'll be asking questions that show them how they are alike and how they are different. As you name the categories, they'll have to decide which circle they will step into. Designate one circle as circle 1, the other as circle 2.

Point out that sometimes the circles of categories overlap, and they'll have to stand in the area where the two circles overlap. For instance, those with brothers will be in one circle, those with sisters in another, and those with both in the overlapping section. Other times, only a few will be able to step into a circles, or only one circle will be occupied. After children understand how the activity works, you may want to give each a turn to name categories. Children should return to the outside of the circles before you name another set of characteristics.

 If your group has many younger children, you can simplify the game by have two separate (rather than overlapping) circles.

Here are sample categories:
- girls in circle 1, boys in circle 2
- those who have socks on, circle 1; those who don't, circle 2
- those with blonde hair, circle 1; all others, circle 2
- those who are wearing something red, circle 1; those who aren't, circle 2
- those who ride the bus to school; those who walk
- those with five or more in their family; those with four or fewer in their family
- those with a brother; those with a sister
- those who like ice cream; those who like pizza
- those who like school; those who like vacation
- those who have a dog; those who have a cat or other pet
- those who like to play sports; those who like to read

As the activity proceeds, be sure to point out that we all are different: the circles keep filling with different people.

Now pick up the strings and say, **Now we'd like to make a circle that includes everyone. I wonder how we could do it?** Invite children to suggest ideas that would solve the problem. Untie the knots and tie the strings together to form one big circle. Lay it on the floor and say, **Which categories can you name so that everyone can get into this one circle?** (Our class; kids who go to school; kids who are invited to be part of God's family; kids who need a Savior; kids God loves.)

Summarize by saying something like the following: **People are different in many ways. But all people everywhere—no matter how different they are—are invited to be part of God's family.**

Pictures of Heaven

Time
15-20 minutes
Materials
☐ Drawing paper
☐ Bright markers
☐ Cake (optional)

Explain that the feast or banquet in today's parable is a picture of what heaven is going to be like. People from every nation and time and place will gather together, celebrating with Jesus. We'll be doing a whole lot more than just eating together, of course!

Invite the children to use their imaginations to think about heaven. When they try to picture heaven in their minds, what does it look like? Have them close their eyes for a minute or so as they try picturing heaven. Ask if anyone wants to share their ideas with the group.

 tip While the children are working, you could serve them cake, explaining that cake is often used as a dessert at banquets.

Then distribute drawing paper and bright markers. Invite the children to draw a picture of what they think heaven will be like. They should make their picture big enough so that it touches all the sides of the paper. When they're finished, those who are willing to do so may show the others their work.

Small Group Session: Grades 4-8

The Great Banquet

Scripture
Matthew 7:24-27

Memory Challenge
Matthew 7:24-27

Focus
Jesus teaches us that God invites all kinds of people to become part of his family (kingdom).

1 HELLO Circle Game

Body Smart   People Smart
Number Smart   Self Smart

Goal
Introduce the idea that we are all different yet all the same in our need for Jesus and in God's love for us.
Time
10-15 minutes
Materials
☐ Two 15' (5 m) lengths of string, twine, or rope

Here's a game that will help kids recognize some of the differences and some of the similarities between them.

Move the chairs and tables to one side or bring everyone outside. Knot the ends of the strings into two loops and position on the floor as shown here:

Gather the kids around the outside of the two rope circles and say that you'll be asking questions that will show them how they are alike and how they are different. As you name the categories, they'll have to decide which circle they will step into. Designate one circle as circle 1, the other as circle 2.

Point out that sometimes they'll have to stand in the area where the two circles overlap. For instance, those with brothers will be in one circle, those with sisters in another, and those with both in the overlapping section. Other times, only a few will be able to step into a circle, or only one circle will be occupied. Everyone should return to the outside of the circles before you name another set of characteristics.

 tip After you've done a few rounds, let the kids name the categories.

Here are some sample categories:
- those who think girls are smarter than boys, circle 1; others, circle 2
- those who can hold the middle three fingers of each hand straight up while thumb and pinkie are touching, circle 1; those who can't, circle 2

- those who have sung a solo in front of a group, circle 1; those who haven't, circle 2
- those with a brother; those with a sister
- those who like ice cream and spinach; those who like pizza and peas
- those who like reading books; those who like science projects
- those who have a dog or cat; those who have another pet
- those who like to play sports; those who play a musical instrument

Untie the knots to form one big circle. Then say something like this: **Now I want you think about categories that relate to our relationship with God. What could we say that would be sure to land each of us in this one circle?** Give them an example to get them started, if necessary:
- all who have sinned
- all who need Jesus as a Savior
- all whom God invites to be in his family
- all whom God loves
- all who can contribute to God's kingdom in some way

Summarize as follows: **People are different in many ways. But all people everywhere—no matter how different they are—are invited to be part of God's family.**

2 KNOW — Dramatization: Contemporary Parable

Word Smart, People Smart, Body Smart

Goal
Tell what Jesus' story teaches about who will be in God's kingdom.

Time
15-20 minutes

Materials
☐ Bibles

Making a contemporary drama of the story of the great banquet will help your kids think through the meaning of the parable.

If possible, involve the entire class in presenting one drama; however, if your class is larger than, say, ten kids, you may want to divide into two smaller groups, each preparing and presenting its own drama. Distribute Bibles and have everyone find the parable of the great banquet (Luke 14:15-24). Ask the group or groups to plan and then act out a modern version of the parable. The skits can be funny and needn't follow the biblical story exactly; however, they should make the same points as the biblical story.

> **tip** If your group has not seen the parable of the great banquet as presented during the large group session, consider reading through the script on pages 141-143. You'll need six or more readers. Give your group a few minutes to look over their lines, then proceed to read through the script; act it out as you read it.

> **tip** Encourage your middle schoolers to act as leaders in the planning of the skit. If you're working only with younger children, you will want to lead the planning yourself, use the simpler option to this step, or have the children act out the story from the Bible rather than make up their own contemporary parable.

Encourage the group to consider these questions as they do their planning (put these on newsprint or on your board):
- What kind of event will we invite people to—a party, an outing, a retreat? Something else? Who's giving it?
- Who shall we send the first invitations to?

- What excuses will the invited people give for not coming?
- How will the person giving the event feel when he or she hears the excuses?
- How will we make sure that people do attend the event?

To keep the dramas somewhat spontaneous, allow no more than ten minutes for the planning, then jump right into the presentations.

After the presentation(s), ask **What is Jesus teaching us in this parable? What do you think he's telling us about who will be in God's family or God's kingdom?** Listen to all responses. You may want to explain the context of the parable (see WordSearch). Note that Jesus was warning the religious leaders who didn't believe in him that if they refused God's invitation, God would reject them and the kingdom would be opened up to other people, the Gentiles. This, of course, is exactly what happened. The invitation to come to God's banquet has now been given to all people everywhere.

You may want to read Revelation 5:9-10 to the group. It's a wonderful picture of the diversity of people gathered before the throne of God.

Option to step 2

Reader's Theater Word Smart

Time
10 minutes

Materials
☐ Bibles

Distribute Bibles and have everyone find Luke 14:16-24. Ask for volunteers to read the following parts (in order of appearance):

 Use this option if you're looking for a simpler, quicker way to review or present today's story.

- narrator (reads all lines not in quotation marks)
- master
- servant
- first excuse-giver
- second excuse-giver
- third excuse-giver

After the reader's theater, ask the same question that concludes the regular step.

 Word Smart People Smart   Self Smart

Top Ten

Goal
Sense the importance of responding to God's invitation.

Time
20 minutes

Materials
☐ Paper, pens

Have kids work in pairs to make a list of the top ten people and invitations to which they would almost certainly say yes. For example, an invitation to visit the president at the White House or to visit the prime minister at Sussex Drive in Ottawa; an invitation to go on a trip to Disney World with a friend; an invitation to a party this weekend at your best friend's house; and so on. Give kids five minutes or so to complete their list.

 Short on time? Have the kids make a top five or top three list.

Then ask one pair to give their number ten statement, the next pair their number nine, and so on. When you get close to number one, sample a few more responses. When all have had a chance to share their statements, and hopefully a few laughs, reflect with the kids on their lists. Ask questions like these:

- **Did anyone mention God or Jesus?** Talk about why God's invitation to join his family is by far the most important invitation any human being can ever receive. It should be number one on everyone's list!
- **As we saw in the parable, God's invitation goes out to everyone. So why do people sometimes say no to God?**
- **How do you think God feels when people ignore the invitation or reject it?**

Affirm that God loves us and wants us to be part of the kingdom. Then talk about what saying yes to Jesus means. You may want to have a time of silent prayer during which the kids can ask Jesus into their hearts and lives or just talk to Jesus about their relationship with him.

Where Am I in This Parable?

Option to step 3

 Self Smart   Body Smart    Word Smart

Time
10 minutes
Materials
☐ "Where Am I in This Parable?" (reproducible page 203), one per student
☐ Pen or pencil

To help kids reflect on their own reaction to God's invitation, distribute copies of "Where Am I in This Parable?" (reproducible page 203). Read the sentence starters to the kids and ask them to think about which response or responses they'd like to check and then complete with their personal thoughts.

Allow five minutes for writing, then invite those who want to share any part of their response to do so. You may want to talk with the kids about what saying yes to Jesus means.

> **tip** Some of your group may be thinking about professing their faith before the congregation. This is one more way to say yes to God. Invite questions on this topic and let kids know you're willing to talk with them about this privately, if they wish to do so.

Conclude this step by having a time of silent prayer, during which each person may talk to God about what he or she wrote. If some have not yet said yes to God's invitation, encourage them to use this moment of prayer to welcome Jesus into their hearts and lives. Open and close the prayer yourself.

4 SHOW
Unit and Session Projects

Goal
Celebrate the diversity of all who accept God's invitation with us.
Time
15-30 minutes
Materials
See individual projects for lists

Below are a variety of projects to help group members apply this parable to their lives. Some of the projects are continuations from the first session and can run for the entire unit; others are for just this week. Choose one or more that best suits your time frame and the interests/abilities of the kids in your group.

Unit Project Ideas

Memorize and Share a Parable

Time
5-15 minutes
Materials
☐ Memory Challenge (reproducible page 183 or 184), one per student
☐ Notecards with each word of Matt. 7:24-25 (see below; 2 sets)
☐ Snack (optional)

If you introduced the challenge of memorizing the parable of the wise and foolish builders in your last session, find out how the group is doing today. Try saying the first two verses of the passage, Matthew 7:24-25, together as a group. Divide the group into two teams. Give each team a set of notecards with the words from these verses written on them, one word per card. Then say, **See how quickly you can put the verses back in the right order!**

Signal time for the teams to begin working. When the first team finishes correctly, you may want to give them a small snack as a prize. When the second team finishes, reward them in the same way. While the group is enjoying their snack, distribute copies of the Memory Challenge and read through verse 26 together. Challenge the group to learn verse 26 before your next session.

Sharable Parable Bookmarks

Time
15-20 minutes
Materials
☐ Bookmark pattern (reproducible page 187)
☐ Crayons
☐ Paper punch
☐ Construction paper, various colors
☐ Glue sticks
☐ Small pieces of ribbon

If the group enjoyed this craft last time, have them repeat it for today's session, coloring or decorating their bookmarks with symbols that reflect today's story. Run copies of the pattern (reproducible page 187) on heavy stock. Kids can either color in the circles or glue on paper-punched circles of various colors of construction paper for a mosaic look.

For today's session, a piece of fruit, a table, or a plate would make an appropriate design. Notice that there's room at the bottom of the bookmark to print a title or the Scripture location of the parable. Attach a ribbon through a hole punched at the top of the bookmark.

Encourage everyone to show the bookmark to their families and friends and to share the parable with them.

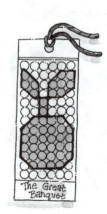

Sun Art Picture Smart   Earth Smart

Time
15-20 minutes per session
Materials
☐ Construction paper in various dark colors
☐ Removable glue sticks (check your local craft store)
☐ Scissors
☐ Toothpicks
☐ Pen

This project, adapted from a Martha Stewart newspaper column, uses the power of the sun to make a unique kind of art. Kids can make interesting illustrations related to the parables they're learning. The basic idea is to place cutout shapes on a sheet of colored construction paper. Cut out shapes from construction paper and glue with removable glue to the sheet. Then tape the sheet, cutouts facing out, to a window where it will catch a lot of sun. After a week or so (longer if higher contrast is desired), peel off the cutouts. The images will be bold and sharp on the construction paper, while the paper surrounding the images has faded in color.

For today's session of the parable of the great banquet, kids could use cutouts or toothpicks to make an outline of a chair and table. Letters can also be used as cutouts for those who want to label their artwork.

Kids can take this project home today, hang it in a sunny window, and let the sun do its work for a week or so. They can add this sun print to the others they've already made, if any. Encourage them to show their art to their family and friends and explain how it relates to the parable of the great banquet.

One-Session Project Ideas

Note: Some of the ideas in this section (Weaving; A Prayer for Openness) came from *Hand in Hand: Helping Children Celebrate Diversity,* Faith Alive Christian Resources. Leaders may want to consult this rich resource for additional ideas. You can order a copy by calling 1-800-333-8300 or visiting www.FaithAliveResources.org.

A Taste of Diversity Body Smart   Picture Smart   People Smart

Time
15-20 minutes
Materials
☐ Smorgasbord of half a dozen or more snacks from a variety of cultures or countries (see examples below)
☐ Small paper plates
☐ Drinks
☐ World globe or map
☐ Song: "The Great Parade" (p.165; CD, track 8)
☐ Balloons and crepe paper (optional)

Here's an opportunity to celebrate diversity with a feast of foods from various cultures and countries. Prior to your meeting, visit the ethnic section of your local grocery store and pick up a variety of, say, half a dozen or more treats from various cultures or countries. See the list below for some ideas.

- tortilla chips (Mexico)
- potato chips (USA)
- fortune cookies or rice crackers or almond cookies (China)
- mango (Africa)
- pita bread (Middle East)
- yogurt (Middle East)
- coffee (South and Central America)
- tea (China, Japan)
- fry bread (Native American)
- Hamantaschen cookies (Jewish)
- Gouda or Swiss Cheese (Holland, Switzerland)
- plantain chips (Caribbean, Costa Rica)

tip Be sure to check ahead of time to see if any members of your group have food allergies. You'll want to exclude those foods from your smorgasboard!

To put the group in a festive mood, you might also want to have them decorate the room with the balloons and crepe paper you supply.

Explain that the various snacks we'll be enjoying come from different countries and cultures. Give everyone the opportunity to identify each snack and its culture of origin. Have them find the country or region of origin on a globe or map. Mention that food is just one item of many that come from cultures and countries other than our own (have the kids give examples of other items, such as cars, computers, shoes, and so on).

Remind the group that in the parable of the great banquet, the host wanted all kinds of people at his banquet. He did not care about their culture or nationality or background or appearance. Someday, when we go to be with Jesus, we will be joined by people from every tribe and nation and time and place—and perhaps we'll enjoy a variety of foods that we can't even begin to imagine!

Conclude by listening to or singing "The Great Parade" (CD, track 8) and/or "Big House" (CD, track 7).

Weaving *Picture Smart   Body Smart   People Smart*

Time
30-45 minutes

Materials
☐ Solid-colored cloth or paper for background pieces, about 9" x 12" (22.5 x 30 cm)
☐ Cloth or paper in various colors and patterns from which 10" x 1" (25 x 2.5 cm) strips can be cut
☐ Scissors
☐ Glue
☐ Ribbon or yarn for hanging weaving (optional)
☐ Dowels, one per person (optional)

Kente cloth is a type of weaving made by the Asante people of Ghana, located in West Africa. Now used by many people, this cloth was once intended only for kings (Alexandra M. Terzian, *The Kids' Multicultural Art Book*, p. 110). It's made by weaving strips of cloth or paper through slits in a background piece of fabric or paper.

Making a piece of *kente* cloth will help to illustrate the theme of diversity and oneness. As your group works, talk about how the individual strips of cloth in the weaving represent the uniqueness of each person. The common background fabric represents the ways that people are alike, bound together by our humanity, by our need for a Savior, and by the love of God who created us.

Show the group a finished piece so they have a clear idea of what they'll be doing. Start by distributing the background pieces. Have the kids cut 1" (2.5 cm) slits in a piece of fabric or paper. Each slit should be an inch apart. Leave an inch between rows.

Next, cut out the individual strips of cloth or paper for the weaving (again, this could be done prior to the session, but it would also be fun for group members to select and cut their own pieces).

 To save lots of time, have a helper or two cut the slits prior to the session. You can also save time by reducing the number of slits on the background piece.

Have the kids weave their strips in and out of the slits.

tip Instead of smaller individual weavings, your group may want to make a single large weaving together. This will take much less time than the individual weavings. To do this, each person should choose a strip of cloth he or she especially likes. The strips can be combined with the background piece to form a piece of *kente* cloth that represents your group. Again, the top edge can be left plain or folded over to form a pocket for a dowel in order to hang it up.

If you wish to hang the completed weaving, fold over the top edge and glue in place, leaving an opening through which the dowel can be slipped. Tie a piece of ribbon or yarn to each end. You could also leave the edge unfinished and place the cloth on a table or dresser top.

Write a Missionary; Take a Field Trip

Word Smart   People Smart   Body Smart

Time
15-20 minutes
Materials
☐ Information (pictures, if possible) about a missionary your congregation sponsors
☐ Paper and pens

Explain that the parable of the great banquet is about inviting everyone we can to join God's family. We do that on a personal level but also as a church when we send out missionaries to places near and far.

Take a few minutes to share pictures and information about a missionary your church sponsors. Then distribute paper and pens and ask the kids to write a short note to that missionary. Suggest that they mention what they've learned from the parable of the great banquet, share a few facts about themselves, and offer encouragement and thanks for the work the missionary is doing. Collect the letters and mail with a brief cover letter of your own.

As an alternative to the above, take your group on a service project to the nearest inner city mission or soup kitchen. Make arrangements for them to help serve the food. Afterwards, talk about what they learned from the experience. You may choose to organize a food or clothing drive as part of your response to this experience. (See session 5 for other service project ideas.)

Invitation Making   Body Smart   People Smart

Time
15-20 minutes
Materials
☐ Cardstock or light-colored construction paper
☐ Old magazines
☐ Scissors
☐ Glue sticks
☐ Bits of felt, ribbon, cut paper, other materials for decorating cards
☐ Markers, colored pencils, crayons
☐ Envelopes

This activity is suggested for kindergarten-grade 3 but could be used at this level if you have kids design invitations to the summer celebration program (assuming you're planning one). Invitations could be sent to relatives, neighbors, or friends. Given the short time frame of many summer programs, it may be necessary to have the kids personally deliver the invitations rather than mail them. If mailing is possible, you will want to provide envelopes for kids to address at home.

Distribute the cardstock or light-colored construction paper and the other materials you've brought. Kids can fold cardstock in half and decorate with cut paper, pictures cut from magazines, or their own illustrations. Be sure to supply them with information regarding the time and place of the celebration so they can compose an accurate (and warm!) invitation.

Provide envelopes for mailing or ask everyone to deliver the invitations by hand.

Story Sequencing Cards

Picture Smart   Number Smart   Word Smart

Time
20-30 minutes
Materials
☐ Story Sequencing Cards (reproducible pages 205-206), photocopied on cardstock, one set per person
☐ Scissors
☐ Crayons, markers, colored pencils
☐ Pencils

This activity is suitable for kids in grades 4 and 5 to make for their own use; older kids can make a set to give to a younger child or use them to tell the parable to a younger child (great for babysitting jobs).

Give a set of story cards to each person. Ask group members to draw a picture that illustrates the written text on each card. It's probably easiest for most kids to make a light pencil outline of the pictures, then color them in. Next, ask kids to cut the cards out. They can mix the cards up and put them back in sequence as they retell the parable to younger siblings at home.

Here's a set of cards drawn by Angie Groenboom, daughter of the authors.

A Prayer for Openness

Word Smart · Body Smart · People Smart

Time
5 minutes

Materials
None needed

This prayer from *Hand in Hand: Helping Children Celebrate Diversity,* offers a powerful way to close today's session. Stand in a circle as you pray. Ask for three volunteer readers, one for each section of the prayer. The readers may read a line, then wait for the others to say it in unison, or simply read the prayer as the others follow the motions and listen. Hand motions are printed in **bold** type.

Clench hands into fists.
Lord, sometimes I want to hurt others
    with my words or with my actions,
especially those who look, talk, and act
    in ways that differ from the way
    that I look, talk, and act.
Forgive me, Lord, for the hatred
    that this clenched fist of mine shows.
Forgive me for wanting to shut others out,
    for shutting you out,
    and for thinking only of myself.

Open hands, palm up.
Open my hands, Lord,
so that I can no longer
    shut you out,
    or shut out my neighbors
    or strike out and hurt others
    with my words or my actions.
Fill these open hands with your love, Lord,
and show them what to do,
    so that I can reach out and help those in need,
    so that I can serve my neighbors.

Join hands with others in circle.
Lord, help me to join hands with others,
with all those in my neighborhood,
    at home, at school, at church,
    and everywhere.
Thank you, Lord, for all these people,
    your people,
    people like me,
    and people different from me.
Thank you, Lord,
    for making all of us,
    and for loving all of us.
Help us to show our love for each other
    and for you. Amen.

Note: You may photocopy this prayer to give to your students to pray at home, if you wish to do so.

Large Group Session

4 The Lost Son

Scripture
Luke 15:11-32

Focus
Jesus teaches us to love and forgive each other the way God loves and forgives us.

WORDSearch

Think About It

I suppose a creative preacher could do a series of sermons on the Prodigal Son and cover a host of life applications: submitting to your father and mother, stewardship, sibling rivalry, and on and on. There are a lot of rabbits to chase in this parable. But one rabbit, above all the others, leads the pack. It's forgiveness.

"I've had it. Get me out of this two-bit town. Gimme my money. See you later." What a way for a son to treat his father! But that's not all. That's just the injury. Here comes the insult. He squanders his wealth (or is it his dad's?) on wild living and prostitutes. He's broke. Finally he comes to his senses. With his tail between his legs (as it should be) he comes running home.

And now here it comes—are you ready? His father sees him a long way off and runs to him. This is no time for walking. His father runs . . . to do what? To take him in his arms, to kiss him, to throw a party, to celebrate, to be glad with him. His father runs to do what? It's obvious, isn't it? He runs to *forgive* his repentant son. What an amazing story. No lecture. No finger pointing. No dwelling on the sincerity of the apology. Just sheer joy that can only burst forth from genuine forgiveness. A truly beautiful scene: the father *runs* to embrace his son.

Why is it so hard for us to forgive like that? Why do we ask questions like Peter did in Matthew 18:21— "Lord, how many times shall I forgive my brother when he sins against me? Up to seven times?" Incidentally, Peter thought he was really walking the extra forgiveness mile here, because Jewish leaders taught their constituency to forgive no more than three times. "I'll even forgive seven times, Lord," Peter seems to be saying. But Jesus demands nothing less than running—not walking—the forgiveness mile. "I tell you, not seven times, but seventy-seven times." In other words, an unlimited amount of forgiveness. Run the extra mile. Don't walk. Run to your brother or sister. Accept him. Forgive her. Don't walk. Run.

Why? You know the answers as well as I do. One of them is that our God forgives. So we must too. "If you, O LORD, kept a record of sins, O LORD, who could stand? But with you there is forgiveness" (Ps. 130:3-4). "If we confess our sins, he is faithful and just and will forgive us our sins and purify us from all unrighteousness" (1 John 1:9). "Be kind and compassionate to one another, forgiving each other, just as in Christ God forgave you" (Eph. 4:32). Like our forgiving God, we must forgive.

Pray About It

Pray that God will use this parable to train you to become a more accepting and forgiving person. Pray for a new spirit of forgiveness in your life. Pray that you will bow in wonder at our merciful and forgiving God. And pray that God will break down any walls that are between you and someone you need to forgive. Pray that the joy of forgiveness will begin bursting into your life and spilling into the lives of those around you.

Tell About It

Tell the children that God, in Jesus Christ, welcomes and accepts and forgives us. That he is filled with joy to do it. And tell the children that forgiveness—asking for it and giving it—needs to be a part of our lives every day. Tell the children that forgiving others will bring them joy. And tell them that we need Jesus' help to do it.

But there's another reason to forgive. Look at the joy in that scene. A father running to embrace, forgive, and accept his son. Instant celebration. Spontaneous joy. And the joy spills *upward* into heaven. Can you fathom that truth? Read the two short parables before the prodigal son—the lost sheep and the lost coin. Both end with repentance and acceptance and forgiveness. And what does Jesus say in both of them? "There is rejoicing in the presence of the angels of God over one sinner who repents." For you see, that repentant sinner has experienced the joy of God's forgiveness. That joy is like nothing else—it splashes upward into heaven so that even the angels may celebrate.

Still not feeling like you can be a forgiving person? Listen, you're in good company. When Jesus tells his disciples they must forgive a brother or sister who repents, not just once or twice, but endlessly, they are aghast. All they can say after hearing this little instruction is: "Lord! Increase our faith!" (Luke 17:4-5). In other words, "We can't do it. We can't forgive like that. We can do the forgiveness walk, but we're just a little too out of shape to do the running version. So increase our faith, Lord."

Need help running to forgive? The good news is that you are a disciple of Christ too. And he is abundantly able and willing to increase your faith. Just ask.

Planning the Session

Today you will teach a parable that is a favorite of many Christians. It's a powerful story of a loving and forgiving Father, a story of amazing grace, a story of forgiveness that has the power to move us and change us.

If you're dramatizing this parable for the summer celebration program, as we suggest, your drama team may want to put a little extra time and effort into their presentation. And bear with us as we remind you again to budget time to review the songs your group has already learned and to learn the new song for this session.

The suggestions in this large group session assume that you'll be dramatizing the parable of the lost son to children and young teens and preparing them to respond to it in small groups.

Singing

By now the kids will be used to singing "Ha La La La" (CD, track 1) as they enter your worship space. You may also want to review "Stop and Let Me Tell You" (track 2), "He Is the Rock" (track 5), and "Big House" (track 7). All four songs are suggested as part of the summer celebration program.

For today's session, we suggest a contemporary update of a classic: "Amazing Grace/Fill It Up" (track 8), also suggested for the summer celebration program. Kids can use the clappers from last session to tap out the beat of this rhythmic song.

Drama

Before presenting "The Lost Son" ask someone—preferably a good middle school reader—to read the parable (Luke 15:11-32) from an easy-to-understand version such as the NIrV or the New Living Bible.

For today's drama you will need the script on pages 145-148 and seven actors. Please see session 1 for general comments regarding drama teams, memorizing lines, and presenting the drama without rehearsal.

Today's skit is a bit unusual in that it takes two of the performers into the aisles of the church (the father and his younger son). That always makes for an extra bit of

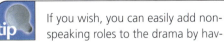
tip If you wish, you can easily add non-speaking roles to the drama by having younger children be on stage as additional "pigs" in the Penelope Porkman/Perez scene and as celebrants at the feast when the lost son comes home. (You will need to rewrite the scene a bit to accommodate this as well as arrange a place on your stage for the celebrative feast; you could cover the desk with a colorful tablecloth to suggest a banquet scene.)

excitement and audience involvement. The stage itself can be kept simple, with a desk and chair to represent dad and home at center stage and a makeshift fence to suggest a pigsty at stage left or right.

Note that the narrator's lines are delivered offstage through the sound system. Coach that performer to read slowly and clearly; emphasize that he or she should not rush the lines.

Costumes should not be a problem, except perhaps for that of the pig, who needs a pink snout and tail and other inventive garb. Props too are simple—a desk and chair, a bucket with banana chips, a suitcase with play money, a hobo's satchel, a fence, a ring and robe. See the skit for details.

Like the other dramas in this course, "The Lost Son" should be a fun production for both performers and audience.

Small Groups

After the drama, children will again meet in small groups. Notice that we've included two session plans—one for children in kindergarten-grade 3 and another for children in grades 4-8. If your regular church school leaders are present, it's probably best to have the children meet in their groups as usual; however, you could also choose to combine several groups together. Each small group leader will need to adapt the plan to the needs of his or her children.

4

Small Group Session: Kindergarten-Grade 3

The Lost Son

Scripture
Luke 15:11-32

Memory Fun
Psalm 119:105

Focus
Jesus teaches us to love and forgive each other the way that God loves and forgives us.

1 HELLO
Game: Hide a Heart

Body Smart
Word Smart

Goal
Introduce the key ideas behind today's parable.

Time
10 minutes

Materials
☐ Construction paper heart with the word *love* on one side and *forgive* on the other

When all the children have arrived, invite them to play a little game called "hide a heart." Choose one child to hide the paper heart anywhere in the room while the others cover their eyes. Once the heart is hidden, the children can look for it or take turns guessing where it might be. Play until everyone who wishes to do so has a chance to hide the heart.

Show the children the two words on the heart (*love* and *forgive*). Ask an older child to read them aloud. Then say them in unison several times. Say something like this: **Suppose a friend is mean to you at school. She pushes you and you fall down and scrape your knees. Later, your friend says she is very sorry. And you say, "That's OK—I forgive you." And you still love that person as your friend.** Ask the children if they can think of a way to *show* love and forgiveness (give someone a hug or a smile).

Explain that in today's parable we learn to love and forgive others just as God loves and forgives us. The parable is about a son who leaves home and finds himself in very big trouble. He needs to be loved and forgiven. Ask the children to watch for how the father in the story shows love and forgiveness.

Option to step 1

Game: Family Fun
Body Smart *Word Smart*

Time
10 minutes

Materials
☐ Large balloon or beach ball with *family* written on it and stick figures to represent a family

Use this option if you want the children to talk about their families as a way into today's story. This will tie in nicely with the "family photo frame" activity (see option to step 4).

Show the children the inflated balloon or beach ball with the word *family* and the stick figures drawn on it. Explain that as they toss the balloon or ball, the person who catches it gets to say something that he or she likes about his or her family. Children who have had a turn should toss the balloon or ball to someone who hasn't yet had a turn.

After the activity, comment that families are great. God made us a part of a family so that we can always be loved and—when we've done something wrong—forgiven. Explain these terms using the example and comments from the regular step.

> **tip:** If you know that some of your children come from broken or dysfunctional families, you may either want to avoid this option or take care to communicate that even though all families have problems and are far from perfect, they still are places where we belong and are loved.

2 KNOW
A Walk Through the Parable

Body Smart, Word Smart, People Smart

Goal
Tell what happened when the younger son came home.

Time
15 minutes

Materials
☐ Two signs: *Home* and *Faraway Land*
☐ Play money (enough for each child to have several bills)
☐ Balloons (optional)

Explain that Jesus once told a story to show how our Father in heaven accepts (loves) and forgives us, and how we are to accept (love) and forgive others. It's the story the children saw acted out in your large group session today! Invite children to tell you what they remember of that story. Then explain that you are going to retell that story to the children—and you want them to help you by acting parts of it out. You will tell them what to do and when to do it.

> **tip:** If the weather is cooperative, you could tell this story outside and separate the two areas by a greater distance.

Using your signs, designate two areas in your room and hallway as "home" and "faraway land."

Begin by gathering the children around you in the "home" area. Explain that a dad and his two sons lived at home. They were farmers and they worked hard in the fields all day long. The father really loved his two sons. One day the youngest son asked his dad for his share of the family money that he would get once the father was dead. This was not a nice thing to do, but he did it anyway. After he got the money, the younger son left home. (**Hand out play money to each child, saying, "Here's your money. I will miss you very much."**)

Explain that the younger son then started walking toward a faraway land. (**Begin walking with your group toward the faraway land.**) Continue along these lines:

The younger son was happy on the way. He danced as he walked and said "yahoo" out loud many times. (**Dance and say "yahoo" with the children**).

When he got to the faraway land, he found lots of friends. (**Have the children shake hands with each other and smile.**) He wasted all of his money on wild parties and having fun. (**Have kids throw money around.**) It wasn't long before all of the money his father had given him was gone! (**Have children hold up empty hands.**)

Now things really got bad. There was not enough food in the faraway land, and the young son got very, very hungry. (**Have kids rub tummy and groan.**) He looked for work to do so he could earn money to buy food. At last he found a job taking care of pigs. As he tossed them their food, he was so hungry that he wanted to eat some himself! (**Have kids make "Oink, Oink" sounds as they pretend to toss feed to pigs.**) But no one gave him anything to eat.

Then the son remembered that his father had plenty of food at home. No one was hungry there! So he decided to go back home. He would tell his father how sorry he was for leaving home and wasting all his money. And so he started down the long road toward home. (**Begin walking with the children toward home.**) He walked and walked and walked for many days.

Then one day he stopped and looked far down the road. (**Have kids stop, put their hands to their eyes, and look toward home**). Who was that running down the road? Could it be? Could it be his father? Yes! It was Dad, running to meet him.

The father ran to his son and gave him a huge hug and a kiss. (**Have the children do a big "group hug" with you.**) Then the son said, "Father, I have sinned against God and against you. I am no longer worthy to be called your son. Just make me like one of your hired workers." But the father accepted (loved) him and forgave him. "Let's go home and celebrate!" he said. So the father and his son walked down the road together, toward home. (**Walk the remaining distance to home with the children.**)

When they got home, the father gave his son a special ring and a handsome robe. "We are going to have a huge banquet," the father said. We are going to celebrate! For this son of mine was lost but now he is found! So they began to celebrate. (**Hand out balloons, if you like, and have the children dance around; then ask them to sit down and listen to the ending of the story**).

But the older son, the one who stayed home, was not happy. He refused to come to the celebration. (**Have kids shake heads and say "no way."**) His father begged him to come. "Everything I have is yours," said the father. But we *have* to celebrate. You see, this brother of yours was lost. And now he is found!

(**Do some quick clean-up of the money and the balloons**).

Help the children reflect a bit on the story by asking questions like these:
- How do you think the father felt when his son left home?
- How do you think the son felt when all money was gone?
- How did the father show that he loved and forgave his son?
- When we do something wrong and we tell God we are sorry, what does God do? (Stress the key words: God loves us and forgives us. It's like our Father runs to meet us and gives us a hug!)
- When someone says they're sorry for doing something mean to us, what does God want us to do?

Option to step 2

Storybook Picture Smart   Word Smart

Time
5-10 minutes

Materials
☐ Storybook, *"The Parable of the Lost Son"* (reproducible pages 207-208), copied and assembled

Assemble a sample storybook before class. Look at the pictures together and either have the children retell the story from the pictures or read it to them.

 Use this option if you're looking for a simpler, quicker way to review or present today's story.

If you have access to a photocopier with enlargement features, you could enlarge the pages to full size, making it easier for the children to see the book as you read it. Or, if you're artistic, copy the simple drawings and text yourself onto full-size pages.

3 GROW
Musical Activity and Drawing

Picture Smart • Music Smart • Word Smart

Goal
Sense how eager God is to accept and forgive us.

Time
20-25 minutes

Materials
☐ Song: "The Great Parade" (p. 165; CD, track 9)
☐ CD player
☐ Drawing paper
☐ Markers or crayons in various colors

Play a round of musical chairs with the children. Place your chairs in a circle, leaving one out so that you're one chair short. Have all the children march around the inside of the circle while you play "The Great Parade" or some other music of your choice. When the music stops, they must quickly find a chair and sit down. The child left in the middle gets to start and stop the CD. Remove one more chair from the circle. Continue until all the children are left in the middle.

tip: If your children are a bit hyper from "walking through" the story in step 2, you may want to skip the musical chairs and go with a simple explanation of how eager God is to accept and forgive us.

Say something like this: **I noticed how *eager* you all were to find a chair! Most of you actually *ran* toward the chairs. Now I want you to think of someone in our story who was very *eager* and who also *ran*.** Affirm that it was the father in the story who eagerly ran to his son.

Explain that God is like the father in the story—God is *eager* to love us and forgive us when we do something wrong.

Distribute drawing paper and markers or crayons. Say something like this: **Let's draw a picture of the father in the story running to meet his son or giving his son a hug. Let's make our picture nice and big, touching the edges of the paper but leaving a little room for writing at the bottom.** After all the children have drawn something, agree on a caption to add to the page, for example, "Our Father is eager to forgive us" (Luke 15:20) or "God loves us" (Luke 15:20). Write your caption out on the board for the children to copy.

Explain that just as God loves us and forgives us when we do something wrong, so God wants us to love and forgive others when they're sorry for what they did. Invite kids to draw a picture of themselves giving a friend or family member a hug. They may use the opposite side of the drawing paper. Again, agree on a caption for the children to copy: "God wants us to forgive others" or "We love and forgive others."

Conclude the step by leading the children in a simple prayer thanking God for loving us and forgiving us and asking God to help us forgive others who hurt us or are unkind to us.

4 SHOW
Unit and Session Projects

Goal
Remember this parable and to thank God for always loving and forgiving us.
Time
15-30 minutes or more
Materials
See individual projects for lists

Below are a variety of projects to help the children apply this parable to their lives. Some of the projects are continuations from the first session and can run for the entire unit; others are for just this session. Choose one or more that best suits your time frame and the interests and abilities of the children.

Unit Project Ideas
Memory Fun AA Word Smart   👁 Picture Smart

Time
5-10 minutes
Materials
☐ Flashlight
☐ Memory Fun (reproducible page 181)

By now the children should be quite familiar with your memory verse. Turn the flashlight on and ask who would like to say the verse first. If you have a volunteer, hand the light to the child and let her say the verse. If no one volunteers, say the verse first yourself, then ask for volunteers! If your children still seem quite uncertain about the verse, try saying it as a group.

Stress again how important it is for us to listen to the words and stories of Jesus. If you are teaching a group of kids who know how to read, you may want to try one or more of the following ways of reviewing the verse:

- *Disappearing verse:* Write the memory verse on your board or on newsprint. Say it together in unison. Then erase or mark over a word or phrase; again, have the children recite the verse in unison and fill in the missing word. Continue until the entire verse has "disappeared."
- *Word cards:* Divide the memory work into short phrases and write these on plain white paper, using markers. Hand the cards out to the children in the correct order, one or two cards per child. Have each child read the words on his or her card, in sequence. Switch positions a time or two. For older children, hand out the cards randomly and let them arrange the cards in the proper sequence.
- *Puzzle:* Write the verse on a large sheet of posterboard. Then cut into puzzle pieces that the children can fit together.

Sharable Parable Bookmarks Picture Smart   Word Smart

Time
15-20 minutes
Materials
☐ Bookmark pattern (reproducible page 187)
☐ Crayons
☐ Paper punch
☐ Construction paper, various colors
☐ Glue sticks
☐ Small pieces of ribbon

If the children have done this craft for every session so far, they'll probably want to continue it for the last two sessions, giving them a complete set of bookmarks for all the "sharable parables."

Run copies of the pattern (p. 187) on heavy stock. Younger children can simply color in the circles to make a picture or design that reminds them of the story. Older children can glue on paper-punched circles of various colors of construction paper for a mosaic look.

For today's session, kids could make a heart as a symbol of the love and forgiveness of God. A winding road or a stick with a hobo's satchel would also be appropriate. So would a stick figure with open, welcoming arms. As with the other bookmarks, there's room at the bottom to print a title or Scripture location of the parable. Attach a ribbon through a hole punched at the top of the bookmark.

Encourage kids to show the bookmark to their families and friends and to share the parable with them.

Storybooks Word Smart   Picture Smart   People Smart

Time
15 minutes
Materials
☐ Storybook, "The Parable of the Lost Son" (reproducible pages 207-208), one set per child
☐ Crayons

Each of the five sessions offers a take-home storybook that kids may share with their family and friends. For today's session, photocopy pages 209-210 and distribute a set to each child. Walk the children through the folding process, offering your help and the help of older children to the little ones in your group.

1. Fold both pages in half horizontally along the dotted lines.

2. Fold both pages in half vertically along the dotted lines.

3. Insert the second set of folded pages into the first set, so that page 3 is opposite page 2.

Have kids print their names on the cover, then color in the pictures. (If short on time, just read the booklet with them, letting them color it at home.) Encourage them to read the story with their family and friends.

One-Session Project Ideas
Thankful Signing Body Smart Word Smart

Time
15-20 minutes
Materials
None needed

Teach the children how to sign two phrases they can use as part of their prayers at home this week: "Thank you, God, for loving me" and "Thank you, God, for forgiving me."

Thank you

Place the tips of the open hands against the mouth and throw them forward, similar to throwing a kiss. (May be made with one hand.)

God

Point the "G" forward in front of you, draw it up and back down, opening the palm that is facing left.

Love, Loving

The "S" hands are crossed at the wrist and pressed to the heart.

Me

Point the right index finger at yourself.

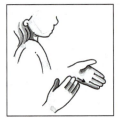

Forgive, Forgiving

Stroke the edge of the left palm with the right fingertips.

—Signs from *The Joy of Signing,* Lottie L. Riekehof, Gospel Publishing House, 1978. Used by permission.

Game: Lost Son Obstacle Course Body Smart

Time
15-20 minutes

Materials
☐ Whistle to signal each turn
☐ Person dressed in robe like the father in the parable
☐ Large box with a house drawn on it (or Little Tykes outdoor playhouse)
☐ Play money
☐ Small box to serve as cash register
☐ Toy stuffed pig (or make your own)
☐ Small wire garden fence
☐ Robe
☐ "Ring pop" suckers, one per child (optional)
☐ Stop watch (optional)

Here's a great way to review the parable and have lots of fun. The obstacle course is best for outdoors, but a large indoor area will work OK too.

First, set up your props in the order of the story (see below), either in a straight line or in a circle. Let the children help you. Then follow these directions:

1. Have the children form one line.
2. At the whistle signal, the first child in line runs to the first obstacle (the house and father) and asks the dad for money. The dad gives the child some play money.
3. The child then runs to the second obstacle (the cash register) where she spends all of her money by putting it in the box.
4. The child runs to the third obstacle (small fenced off area with pig) and jumps into the fenced-off area. She says to the stuffed pig, "I'm so hungry!"
5. The child runs back to the first obstacle (the house and father), where Dad now waits with open arms. The child puts on the robe and (optionally) the ring-pop sucker. The child takes off the robe (for the next person's turn) and runs to the back of the line.
6. The game continues until everyone in the line has had a turn.

tip: If you have children in your group who are not physically able to run the obstacle course, let them serve as observers who make sure the runners actually do what they're supposed to do at each obstacle. They can also serve as timekeepers and help you set up the game.

If you wish, divide kids into two teams and see which team gets through the course in the least time (use the stop watch). We suggest timing teams, not individuals!

Family Photo Frames

People Smart   Self Smart   Picture Smart   Body Smart

Time
20-30 minutes

Materials
☐ Parable of the Lost Son story card (reproducible page 209), one per child
☐ Colorful cardstock (heavy paper)
☐ Posterboard
☐ Scissors
☐ Ruler
☐ Pencil
☐ Craft knife
☐ Glue
☐ Crayons/markers
☐ Yarn
☐ Heavy-duty tape
☐ Felt, fabric scraps
☐ Wiggle eyes

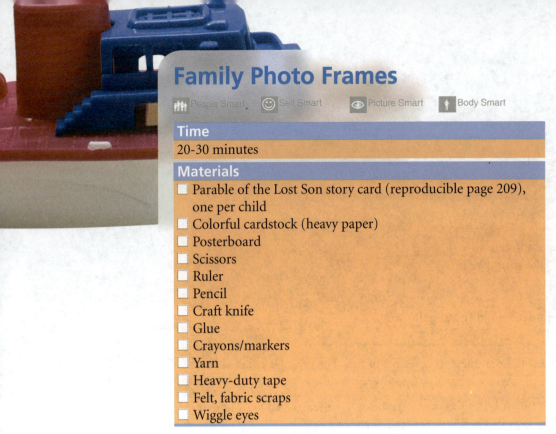

The family is the place where young children experience acceptance and forgiveness on a daily basis. This craft produces an attractive photo frame that shows the uniqueness of each child's family. The front of the finished frame looks something like this:

Notice that the frame itself is decorated with felt or fabric pieces or drawings that represent family faces, pets, and activities. The inside of the frame is blank; here children can insert an actual picture of their family.

> **tip** Be sensitive to the children in your group. If you know or suspect that some of them come from very troubled or broken families, you may want to avoid this activity.

The backside of the frame features a copy of the Parable of the Lost Son. It looks like this:

Prior to today's session, prepare materials as follows:

- Using 8.5 x 11 sheets of cardstock, make copies of the parable story card (reproducible page 209) for each child.
- Use the cardstock as a pattern. Trace around it on the poster board.
- Mark a 2" border on the posterboard and cut out the middle of the posterboard with a craft knife.

tip Think twice before you do all this yourself. Is there someone who could lend you a hand? Perhaps there's a member of the congregation who can't be in the classroom every week but who wouldn't mind helping out from time to time.

During the session, walk the children through these steps. (Be ready to assist your little ones throughout this process, and remember that having a helper in the classroom will make things go a lot better!)

tip Having a finished model ready to show the children will get them excited about doing this craft and will help them visualize the final product.

1. Apply glue to the back (non-shiny) side of the poster frame.
2. Press the cardstock onto the frame, making sure that the story is showing (face up). The story becomes the back side of the frame.
3. Decorate the front of the frame, using crayons, markers, felt or fabric scraps, wiggly eyes, and so on. Encourage the children to make family faces, pets, and pictures of things the family does together.
4. Tape a piece of yarn to the back of the frame so it's ready to hang on a wall (optional).

At home kids can add a family photo to the frame, mounting it directly onto the cardstock with tape, a glue stick, or photo mounting tape. (Or they can draw a picture of their family in the blank space.) Encourage kids to share the story of the lost son and talk about love and forgiveness they find (and give) in their own families.

Snack: Heart-Shaped Cookies Body Smart

Time
5 minutes
Materials
☐ Heart-shaped cookies
☐ Cold drinks

Kids are bound to enjoy this treat while they're working on any of these projects. As you serve the cookies, tell the kids they're a reminder to show love, acceptance, and forgiveness to others.

Small Group Session: Grades 4-8

4 The Lost Son

Scripture
Luke 15:11-32

Memory Challenge
Matthew 7:24-27

Focus
Jesus teaches us to love and forgive each other the way God loves and forgives us.

1 HELLO
Body Smart

Game: Lost

Goal
Introduce the parable of the lost son by sensing what it's like to be "lost."
Time
10 minutes
Materials
☐ Blindfold

When all have arrived, form a large circle of eight to a dozen kids (if you're got a small group, see the option on p. 97). Ask for a volunteer to be blindfolded and stand in the middle of the circle. Have the other kids on the perimeter hold hands and stretch out, leaving only a small opening in one part of the circle.

The blindfolded person in the middle must find that small opening, which you can call "home." Those on the edge of the circle can encourage or discourage the walker or give accurate directions or false directions, as they wish. Stop the walk after one minute, if the walker hasn't found "home."

After several volunteers have tried the walk, ask them what it felt like to be in the circle, looking for "home." Was there a sense of confusion, or being lost? Bridge to the title of today's parable, "The Lost Son," and explain that the son too must have felt "lost" after he left home and spent all his money in a faraway land. He was alone and without friends, wandering around, looking for food and shelter. Finally he decided to end his wandering and come home.

What Would Jesus Say to You?

 Word Smart   Self Smart

Option to step 1

Goal
Introduce the parable of the lost son by reflecting on how God (Jesus) sees us.
Time
10 minutes
Materials
Paper and pens

Use this option if your group is too small for the circle game in the regular step or if your kids are older, more refective, and enjoy writing.

Distribute paper and pens and ask the kids to write an answer to this question: **If Jesus were to step out of a car and walk up to you, what would he say to you?** There's no need for a long response—three minutes should be enough time.

Ask for volunteers to share their answers. Then comment that if they went to a mall and asked ten adults this question, many would probably imagine that Jesus would say something to make them feel guilty. "He'd say I should try harder." Or "He'd tell me to pray more." You might ask for a show of hands of those who think Jesus might just say something like that to them.

Comment that today's parable is about how God really sees us—not just while we're attending church or Sunday school or while we're praying, but also after we've really messed up big time, after we've done something that would get us grounded for a month or a whole lot more. The really amazing thing is that God doesn't condemn us or reject us as worthless. Keith Stulp puts it this way:

> Fortunately for us, the God of the Bible doesn't see it that way. The God of the Bible (shown to us in the person of Jesus) loves us way too much. Our God doesn't stand around with arms crossed tightly, tapping his foot with an angry scowl as we constantly screw up. If anything, God looks hurt and grieved when we mess up—not so much for himself but for us. And when we come back to our senses, he's ready to throw a party!

—*31 More Great Bible Studies,* Faith Alive Christian Resources, p. 59

2 KNOW
Portraits: Father and Older Brother

Word Smart Number Smart Picture Smart People Smart

Time
15-20 minutes
Materials
☐ Bibles
☐ Newsprint
☐ Markers in various colors
☐ Tape

Distribute Bibles and ask everyone to find Luke 15:11-32. Review the parable that was dramatized in the large group presentation by reading it in "reader's theater" fashion. Ask for volunteers to read the following parts:
- narrator (everything not in quotation marks)
- younger son
- father

97

- servant
- older brother

After the reading, divide into groups of two to four kids. Give each group a sheet of newsprint and markers. Have half of the groups draw a sketch of the father; than add words that describe him around the sketch. The other groups should draw a sketch of the older brother with words that describe him. If they wish, they can choose marker colors that suggest the words that describe their character; for example, bright yellow for loving; green for jealousy, red for anger; and so on.

> **tip:** If your group has not seen the parable of the lost son as presented during the large group session, consider reading through the script on pages 145-148. You will need seven or more actors. Give your group a few minutes to look over their lines, then proceed to read through the script and act it out as you read it.

Have the groups display their portraits and read their word lists to the group. What did they discover?

3 GROW

Word Smart, Number Smart, Picture Smart, People Smart

Role Plays: In Need of Forgiveness!

Goal
Realize that God expects us to forgive and accept others the way the father does.

Time
20 minutes

Materials
None needed

Ask kids who Jesus wants us to think about when we hear about the loving father in this story. Have them look again at the list of the character traits they listed next to the portrait of the father. Does this describe the way God is with us when, like the younger brother, we have run away from him and are in need of forgiveness? Does it describe the way God is with us when, like the older brother, we are jealous and unforgiving and self-righteous? Affirm that it does! Just as the father in the parable runs to hug and forgive his lost son, God rushes to forgive us and welcome us home when we are sorry for what we've done wrong.

Comment that in many places in the Bible we are told to forgive others. Because God has so graciously forgiven us, God expects us to forgive—and lovingly accept—others. Divide into groups of two or three, and ask each group to act out one situation in which they would need to forgive someone who has hurt them in some way. If necessary, give them an example or two to get them thinking:

- a friend lies to you about something important
- someone says mean things about you
- a parent or teacher accuses you of doing something wrong that you didn't do
- your little brother or sister spills juice at breakfast all over your new sweater
- someone in the family deletes your book report from the computer; it's due tomorrow
- a bully hits you on the school bus

> **tip:** You might want to write these and similar situations on notecards for kids to act out, especially if you're teaching younger children in grades 4-5.

After each presentation, ask kids how they could go about forgiving the person who hurt them or offended them. At times granting forgiveness may be as simple as saying "I forgive you" or "That's OK" after the person who hurt you says he or she is sorry. Then reconciliation can take place and the relationship can get back to normal. At other times, however, the offending person may never apologize, or the offense may be a very serious one. Help kids see that, like the father, they can't force the offending person to seek forgiveness or to restore their relationship. But they can always patiently pray for that person's well-being and hope for the opportunity to show them forgiveness.

Where Am I in This Parable?

Option to step 3

 Self Smart   Body Smart   Word Smart

Time
10 minutes
Materials
☐ "Where Am I in This Parable?" (reproducible page 211), one copy per person
☐ Pen or pencil

Use this option for a more personal and reflective approach to openness and forgiveness. Hand out copies of "Where Am I in This Parable" and read the sentence starters aloud. Ask kids to take a few minutes to complete all the statements with their personal thoughts.

Allow five minutes for writing, then invite kids to share their responses if they wish to. You may also want to talk a bit about how Jesus told this parable to good, "religious" people who, like the older brother, were not ready to accept and love others they thought were somehow beneath them. They thought that they—and they alone—were the ones loved by God. Wonder with the kids if we ever have that kind of "I'm better than you" attitude toward others.

If the mood seems right, invite the kids to pray silently, asking for God's forgiveness for sometimes not being loving and forgiving to others, and praying for a person they need to forgive (see last two items on reproducible page).

4 SHOW
Unit and Session Projects

Goal
Accept and affirm each other.
Time
15-30 minutes or more
Materials
See individual projects for lists

Below are a variety of projects to help kids apply this parable to their lives. Some of the projects are continuations from the first session and can run for the entire unit, others are for just this week. Choose one or more that best suits your time frame and the interests and abilities of your group.

Unit Project Ideas
Memorize and Share a Parable 　AA Word Smart

Time
5-10 minutes per session
Materials
☐ Bibles
☐ Memory Challenge (reproducible page 183 or 184), one copy per person
☐ Chalkboard/chalk or newsprint/markers

Last time we suggested kids learn Matthew 7:26, part of the parable of the wise and foolish builders. Have them say that verse in unison now.

Before the session print verse 27, today's new verse, on board or newsprint. Read the verse together, commenting that it's the last verse of the parable. When they've learned this verse, they'll know the whole parable!

Challenge the group to begin learning the verse now by using the disappearing word strategy described in session 3. Say the verse together in unison. Then erase or mark over a word or phrase; again, have the group recite the verse in unison and fill in the missing word. Continue until the entire verse has "disappeared."

If you have still more time, try rehearsing the entire passage together. One way to do that is to have the kids pair off and say the parable to each other.

Sharable Parable Bookmarks 👁 Picture Smart AA Word Smart

Time
15-20 minutes
Materials
☐ Bookmark pattern (reproducible page 187)
☐ Crayons
☐ Paper punch
☐ Construction paper, various colors
☐ Glue sticks
☐ Small pieces of ribbon

If your group has done this craft for every session so far, they'll probably want to continue it for the last two sessions, giving them a complete set of bookmarks for all the "sharable parables."

Run copies of the pattern (p. 187) on heavy stock. Kids can either color in the circles to make a design or glue on paper-punched circles of various colors of construction paper for a mosaic look.

For today's session, kids could make a heart as a symbol of God's love and forgiveness. A winding road or a stick with hobo's satchel would also be appropriate. As with the other bookmarks, there's room at the bottom to print a title or the Scripture location of the parable. Attach a ribbon through a hole punched at the top of the bookmark.

Encourage kids to show the bookmark to their families and friends and to share the parable with them.

Sun Art Picture Smart   Earth Smart

Time
15-20 minutes
Materials
☐ Construction paper in various dark colors
☐ Removable glue sticks (check your local craft store)
☐ Scissors
☐ Toothpicks
☐ Pen

This project, adapted from a Martha Stewart newspaper column, uses the power of the sun to make a unique kind of art. Kids can make interesting illustrations related to the parables they're learning. The basic idea is to place cutout shapes on a sheet of colored construction paper. Cut shapes from construction paper and glue with removable glue to the sheet. Then tape the sheet, cutouts facing out, to a window where it will catch a lot of sun. After a week or so (longer if higher contrast is desired), peel off the cutouts. The images will be bold and sharp on the construction paper, while the paper surrounding the images has faded in color.

For today's session on the parable of the lost son, kids could make a winding path or a toothpick stick figure with a hobo satchel, or they could use their own (better!) ideas. Letters can also be used as cutouts for those who want to label their artwork.

Kids can take this project home today, hang it in a sunny window, and let the sun do its work for a week or so. Encourage them to show their art to their family and friends and explain how it relates to the parable of the lost son.

One-Session Project Ideas
Thankful Signing Body Smart   Word Smart

Time
15-20 minutes
Materials
None needed

Teach kids how to sign several phrases they can use as part of their prayers at home this week:
- Thank you, God, for loving me.
- Thank you, God, for forgiving me.
- Thank you, God, for accepting me.
- Teach me to accept and love and forgive others.

Thank you

Place the tips of the open hands against the mouth and throw them forward, similar to throwing a kiss. (May be made with one hand.)

God

Point the "G" forward in front of you, draw it up and back down, opening the palm that is facing left.

Love, Loving

The "S" hands are crossed at the wrist and pressed to the heart.

Me

Point the right index finger at yourself.

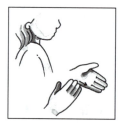   

Forgive, Forgiving

Stroke the edge of the left palm with the right fingertips.

Accept, Accepting

The open "AND" hands point toward each other, palm facing the body. Move hands toward chest, closing them into the "AND" position, fingers touching the body.

Teach

Place both open "AND" hands in front of the forehead facing each other; bring them forward, away from the head, into closed "AND" positions.

Others

Move the "A" hand slightly up and to the right, turning the thumb up and over toward the right.

—Signs from *The Joy of Signing*, Lottie L. Riekehof, Gospel Publishing House, 1978. Used by permission.

Game: Lost Son Obstacle Course   Body Smart   People Smart

Time
15-20 minutes
Materials
☐ Whistle to signal each turn
☐ Person dressed in robe like the father in the parable
☐ Large box with a house drawn on it (or Little Tykes outdoor playhouse)
☐ Play money
☐ Small box to serve as cash register
☐ Toy stuffed pig (or make your own)
☐ Small wire garden fence
☐ Robe
☐ "Ring pop" suckers, one per child (optional)
☐ Stopwatch (optional)

Here's a great way to review the parable and have lots of fun. The obstacle course is best for outdoors, but a large indoor area will work OK too.

First, set up your props in the order of the story (see below), either in a straight line or a circle. Let kids help you. "Sell" the game to this age group as something that's crazy and fun. Then follow these directions:

1. Have kids form one line.
2. At the whistle signal, the first person in line runs to the first obstacle (the house and father) and asks the dad for money. The dad gives him some play money.
3. The person then runs to the second obstacle (the cash register) where he spends all of his or her money by putting it in the box.
4. The person runs to the third obstacle (small fenced off area with pig) and jumps into the fenced-off area. He says to the stuffed pig, "I'm so hungry!"
5. The person runs back to the first obstacle (house and father), where dad now waits with open arms. He puts on the robe and (optionally) the ring-pop sucker. He takes off the robe (for the next person's turn) and runs to the back of the line.
6. The game continues until everyone in the line has had a turn.

For kids in this age group, add some fun by dividing into two teams. Use the stopwatch to see which team can get through the course in the least time (we suggest timing teams, not individuals). Also, let older kids devise some additions of their own to the obstacle course. If some of your middle schoolers feel the game is beneath their dignity, tell them not to be "elder brothers"—they should join in the fun! Or have them help organize the game for the younger children.

If you have children in your group who are not physically able to run the obstacle course, let them serve as observers who make sure the runners actually do what they're supposed to do at each obstacle. They can also serve as timekeepers and help you set up the game.

Community/Acceptance/Affirmation Circle

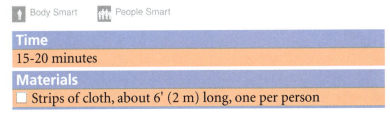

Time
15-20 minutes
Materials
☐ Strips of cloth, about 6' (2 m) long, one per person

Note: This activity comes from *Hand In Hand: Helping Children Celebrate Diversity* (Faith Alive Christian Resources, p. 90).

Stand in a circle with the kids facing toward the center of the circle. Give each person a strip of cloth. Designate one person to begin the activity. She holds one end of the cloth in one hand while giving the other end to someone else in the circle, but not to someone standing directly next to him or her. That person will hold his piece of cloth by the other hand and name someone to take the other end. The process continues until everyone is connected into a web. Each person will have a strip in each hand. Jiggle the web a little or have one person give a tug and see what happens. Observe that what affects one person affects another, or possibly the whole web. Talk about what it means to be a community and part of the same web.

While remaining in the web, you and the group can demonstrate acceptance toward one another. Designate yourself as a beginning point. You are to tell the person holding the other end of your strip one or two things that you value about him or her. The receiver then tells the person holding the other end of his or her strip one or two things she values about that person. The pattern continues around the web until everyone has been enfolded in the web of acceptance and affirmation.

A Prayer for Openness

Word Smart · Body Smart · People Smart

Time
5 minutes

Materials
None needed

This prayer from *Hand in Hand: Helping Children Celebrate Diversity* was suggested last time; however, it fits today's session as well. Kids will benefit from repeating the prayer.

Stand in a circle as you pray. Ask for three volunteer readers, one for each section of the prayer. The readers may read a line, then wait for the others to say it in unison, or simply read the prayer as the others follow the motions and listen. Hand motions printed in **bold** type.

Clench hands into fists.
Lord, sometimes I want to hurt others
   with my words or with my actions,
especially those who look, talk, and act
   in ways that differ from the way
   that I look, talk, and act.
Forgive me, Lord, for the hatred
   that this clenched fist of mine shows.
Forgive me for wanting to shut others out,
   for shutting you out,
   and for thinking only of myself.

Open hands, palm up.
Open my hands, Lord,
so that I can no longer
   shut you out,
   or shut out my neighbors
   or strike out and hurt others
   with my words or my actions.
Fill these open hands with your love, Lord,
and show them what to do,
   so that I can reach out and help those in need,
   so that I can serve my neighbors.

Join hands with others in circle.
Lord, help me to join hands with others,
with all those in my neighborhood,
   at home, at school, at church,
   and everywhere.
Thank you, Lord, for all these people,
   your people,
   people like me,
   and people different from me.
Thank you, Lord,
   for making all of us,
   and for loving all of us.
Help us to show our love for each other
   and for you. Amen

Note: You may photocopy this prayer to give to the children to pray at home, if you wish to do so.

Good Snack, Good Talk Body Smart

Time
10 minutes
Materials
☐ Heart-shaped cookies
☐ Cold drinks (optional)

Hand out the cookies and tell kids they're a reminder of the loving heart of God our Father and how God also wants us to have loving, accepting, and forgiving hearts for others.

While the kids are munching, remind them of the picture of the loving Father in the parable. Go around the circle and invite kids to mention one or two ways they have recently experienced God's love. Conclude by having someone read 1 John 4:19: "We love because he first loved us."

5 — Large Group Session
The Good Samaritan

Scripture
Luke 10:25-37

Focus
Jesus teaches us who our neighbors are and tells us that we should love them.

WORD Search

Think About It

As with most of Jesus' parables, the Good Samaritan is a snapshot of what life is supposed to be like in the kingdom of God. Jesus simply shows us a picture of a loving neighbor tending to his bitter enemy. But let's plumb the depths of this parable by digging around in a few other places in the Word of God.

For instance, do you remember the remarkable event that took place in the upper room? The day before he was crucified, Jesus demonstrated love for his disciples by washing their feet. He then instructed them to do the same to others, following his example (John 13:14).

This poignant picture of our Savior and King humbly washing feet eventually leads to some good strong theology about sanctification (becoming holy or Christlike in our walk of faith). For example, John tells us that the Christian life is all about love, and love works itself out with actions (1 John 3:18). James, the brother of Jesus, follows this up with his famous saying: "faith without deeds is dead" (James 2:26). These words are a rallying cry for sanctification.

Paul picks up the theme: "As we have opportunity, let us do good to all people, especially to those who belong to the family of believers"(Gal. 6:10). Hearing this, we nod our heads in agreement. We like the idea of doing good, especially to *believers.* Simple, we say, they're family.

James also gives us an idea of who to love with our actions: "Religion that God our Father accepts as pure and faultless is this: to look after orphans and widows in their distress" (James 1:27). Orphans? Widows? That's practically easier done than said. A piece of cake. Whose heart doesn't go out to orphans and widows? We'll get right to work on that. Not one complaint is heard.

But the parable of the good Samaritan pushes the "who is my neighbor?" envelope. We hear ourselves balking—"You want me to tend to the needs of my . . . (gulp) . . . enemies?"

"Precisely," says Jesus in his Sermon on the Mount. "You have heard that it was said, 'Love your neighbor and hate your enemy.' But I tell you: Love your enemies" (Matt. 5:43-44).

Not that this was a new idea. Proverbs 25:21 says it plainly enough: "If your enemy is hungry, give him food to eat; if he is thirsty, give him water to drink." Jesus was simply instructing—by first-century show and tell—what his Father had taught from day one. None of this

> **Pray About It**
> Pray that God will use this parable to teach you something about love in action. Pray that your love working itself out in deeds will begin to target believers and unbelievers alike. Pray for a new attitude of generous, abounding love in your heart that extends even to those who, for you, are so difficult to love. Pray that the children you teach will learn to love as God would have them love.

> **Tell About It**
> Tell the children that God has shown love to them through Jesus Christ. Tell them that we show thanks to Jesus by loving others and by doing kind things for them. Tell the children that God wants us to show kindness to the people in our lives that are easy to love and also to those that are hard to love. Tell them that Christ lives in each one of them and will help them to show love in action to everyone.

"enemy loving" was lost on the apostle Paul either. Paul writes: "Bless those who persecute you; bless and do not curse"(Rom. 12:14).

Of course, precisely here is where the whole enterprise gets rather tricky. We think: "I can handle loving my neighbor and caring for widows and orphans, but enemies? That's another story."

But God says, "No, it's not another story. It's my story and your story, dear one." Remember? "You see, at just the right time, when we were still powerless, Christ died for the ungodly. . . . God demonstrates his own love for us in this: while we were still sinners, Christ died for us. . . . When we were God's enemies, we were reconciled to him through the death of his Son. . . . Through our Lord Jesus Christ . . . we have now received reconciliation" (Rom. 5:6-11). God reminds us that his "love in action" began while we were yet his enemies. And God says that, just like him, we must love our enemies.

The parable of the good Samaritan says all that . . . and more. It says, do good to all people. Believers? Of course. Orphans and widows? Sure. But don't forget those enemies of yours who live in a world of hurt and are dying—dying for the healing hands of Christ to bandage the wounds caused by their own sin. Don't forget to be a Samaritan for these enemies. Don't forget to be the hands of Christ for the ones who are the way we used to be.

Planning the Session

Today we end this unit with a powerful reminder to love others, even those we may find very hard to love. It's a theme that we've heard before in this unit—all sorts of folks get invited to the great banquet, and the older brother must learn to show the father's compassion and love to a younger bro who doesn't quite measure up. So we'll be picking up a familiar theme. Leaders of small groups may want to look back at sessions 3 and 4 to see if there are any activities they missed because they ran out of time but might still want to include in their small group sessions today.

If you're presenting a summer celebration program, this may be your last chance to rehearse the songs the children have learned. Be sure to budget some extra time for this review. If some songs aren't being sung by the entire group, perhaps these could be practiced during part of the small group meeting time.

The suggestions in this large group session assume that you'll be dramatizing the parable of the good Samaritan to children and young teens and preparing them to respond to it in small groups.

Singing

Here's a list of the songs we've suggested the children learn during this unit:
- "Ha La La La"
- "Stop and Let Me Tell You"
- "He Is the Rock"
- "Big House"
- "Amazing Grace/Fill It Up"

Of course you can vary this list as you wish. All of the above songs are suggested for the celebration program and can be found on the CD that accompanies this course.

For today's session, we include two songs: the familiar "Jesu, Jesu, Fill Us with Your Love" (p. 168; CD, track 10) and "The Good Samaritan" (p. 169; CD, track 11). Take your choice or do them both, as time and the musical abilities of your kids suggest. "Jesu, Jesu" is also suggested for the summer celebration program.

Optional songs for this session include "You Shall Love the Lord" (p. 176; CD, track 15) by Frank Hernandez and "Make Me a Servant" (p. 178; CD, track 16).

Drama

Before presenting "The Good Samaritan" ask someone—preferably a good reader from your middle school—to read the parable from Luke 10:25-37 using an easy-to-understand version such as the NIrV or New Living Bible.

For today's drama you will need the script on pages 149-152 and six actors. Please see session 1 for general comments regarding drama teams, memorizing lines, and presenting the drama without rehearsal.

Like the biblical story, the setting for the dramatization is simple and stark—a desert road and something behind which your two robbers can wait in ambush. If you wish, you can suggest a path by outlining it with some rocks and plants, but that's strictly optional. The one "odd" prop that's suggested is a fake rock, available from a costume or prop shop or perhaps a landscape store. If you can't find a fake rock (which one of the robbers uses to render the traveler unconscious), substitute another weapon, such as a club, or just have the robber pretend to hit the traveler with his hands.

For the other dramas in this series, we suggested ways to add nonspeaking roles that would allow younger children to participate in the action. Today's drama doesn't seem to allow much expansion beyond six characters, unless you want to add some bandits to plot with Moe and Megs, then remain out of sight until after the robbery, when they can run off the stage with the two main robbers. This seems a bit of a stretch, though, and you're probably better off limiting this last production to a cast of six.

Costumes can be traditional or contemporary, or a happy blend of both. (The skit uses the biblical characters who wear sandals but has the priest consulting a watch and has the Samaritan carrying a Bible, so there's lots of flexibility here!)

If you've had a drama team present the five skits, be sure to have them take a curtain call at the end of today's skit. Include not only all the performers but also those who helped with the sets, costumes, and props. Have the kids give them a standing ovation.

Small Groups

After the drama, children will again meet in small groups. Notice that we've included two session plans—one for children in kindergarten-grade 3 and another for children in grades 4-8. If your regular church school leaders are present, it's probably best to have the children meet in their groups as usual; however, you could also choose to combine several groups together. Each small group leader will need to adapt the plan to the needs of his or her children.

Small Group Session: Kindergarten-Grade 3

The Good Samaritan

Scripture
Luke 10:25-37

Memory Fun
Psalm 119:105

Focus
Jesus teaches us who our neighbors are and tells us we should love them.

1 HELLO *Body Smart* *Word Smart*
Toss the Ball and Name a Neighbor

Goal
Introduce the key idea taught by the parable of the good Samaritan.
Time
10 minutes
Materials
☐ People poster from session 1

When all the children have arrived, say something like this: **Once there was a man who asked Jesus a question that may seem a little strange to you: Who is my neighbor? You see, Jesus had just told this man that he ought to love God and love his neighbor. So the man asked Jesus, "Well, who is my neighbor?" Jesus had a very surprising answer. He didn't say, "Just the people you like" or "Just the people who live in your neighborhood" or "Just the people who go to your church" or "Just the people who are nice to you." No. Jesus told a story that shows that *everyone* is our neighbor. We are supposed to show love and be kind to *everyone*.**

Ask the children to stand in a circle. Toss a beach ball to each other. Whoever throws the ball aims it at someone and says, "[Name], you're my neighbor." Repeat until all kids have had at least a couple of turns. Then change the rules: each person who catches the ball gets to name a neighbor—someone in his or her family, neighborhood, school, or church.

tip If you wish, show the children the people poster from session 1 and remind them that all the different kinds of people shown on the poster are our neighbors, even though we don't know their names or where they live.

Say again that today's story—the parable of the good Samaritan—is a story Jesus told to teach us that everyone is our neighbor, someone we should love and be kind to.

2 KNOW
Story Drama

Goal
Tell what happened to the man who was hurt.

Time
15 minutes

Materials
☐ Good Samaritan puppets (reproducible pages 215-216), prepared ahead of time (for instructions see First Aid Kit activity, pp. 117-118)

Take out your "first aid kit" filled with story figures. Tell the children the puppets in this box are the very same characters the children watched in the drama in your big group meeting today. Introduce each of the characters:

- traveler
- robbers
- priest
- Levite
- Samaritan
- innkeeper

Then ask volunteers to take these puppets and use them to help you retell the story of the good Samaritan. The story outline follows:

1. A man was going down the road from Jerusalem to Jericho. *(Have the traveler slowly walk down the road.)*
2. Suddenly, robbers jumped out from behind the rocks and attacked the traveler. *(Robbers jump out and pretend to hit the traveler.)*
3. The robbers took his money and left him, half-dead, on the side of the road. *(Robbers leave; traveler falls to floor and lies still.)*
4. A priest happened to be walking down that same road. *(Start your priest walking.)* He saw the man who was hurt. But he did not stop. He just walked right by and pretended not to see him. *(Priest walks by.)*
5. Along came a Levite, another important man. *(Start your Levite walking.)* He saw the man who was hurt. But he did not stop. He just walked right by and pretended not to see him. *(Levite walks by.)*
6. Then along came a Samaritan. *(Start the Samaritan down the road).* Usually Jews, like the man who was hurt, did not like Samaritans at all. But when the Samaritan saw the wounded man, he stopped and felt sorry for him. He bent down and began bandaging the man's wounds.
7. The Samaritan helped the wounded man up. *(Pause to let your Samaritan do this.)* He put him on a donkey and brought him to an inn. *(Samaritan pretends to hold a rope while the traveler rides an imaginary donkey.)*

After you have retold the story together, regroup the children and ask questions like these:

- I'm going to ask you the same question Jesus asked after he told this story. Who do you think was a neighbor to the person who was hurt?
- What did the Samaritan do that showed he thought of the wounded man as his neighbor?
- Why would it be especially hard for the Samaritan to help the man who was hurt?

> **tip:** Younger children may not have a clue here, depending on whether or not they picked up the comments written into the retelling, above. You may end up explaining the whole Jew/Samaritan business, but that's OK. The point to make is that the Samaritan wasn't helping a friend—he was helping someone who was an enemy, someone he would usually not like and someone who would not like him at all!

- How do you think the wounded man felt when the priest and the Levite walked right on without stopping to help him? How do you think he felt when the Samaritan helped him?
- Who does Jesus want us to be neighbors to? Who does he want us to show love and kindness to?

Option to step 2

Storybook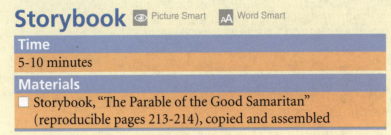

Time
5-10 minutes

Materials
☐ Storybook, "The Parable of the Good Samaritan" (reproducible pages 213-214), copied and assembled

Assemble a sample storybook before class. Either let the children retell the story by looking at the pictures in the book, or read the story as the children look at the pictures together.

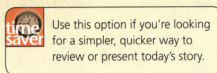
Use this option if you're looking for a simpler, quicker way to review or present today's story.

If you have access to a photocopier with enlargement features, you could enlarge the pages of the storybook to full size, making it easier for the children to see the book as you read it. Or, if you're artistic, copy the simple drawings and text yourself onto full-size pages.

3 GROW
Song and Prayer Chains

Goal
To want to be more loving to others.

Time
15-20 minutes

Materials
☐ Song: "Jesu, Jesu, Fill Us with Your Love" (p. 168; CD, track 10)
☐ CD player
☐ Paper
☐ Scissors
☐ Pens or pencils

Wonder with the children if there are ways that we can be more loving to others. Share with them an example from your own life of how you could be more caring to someone. Ask, **Do you have any ideas about how we can be more loving to others? How about doing things without complaining when Mom or Dad or a teacher asks us to? Could we give Grandma or Grandpa an extra hug sometimes? Could we sometimes say "I love you" to Mom or Dad? Could we give little brother or sister a hug when they're crying?** Wonder with the children along these lines, and listen to their own ideas.

Point out that one thing we can all do is to ask Jesus to fill us with his love. Ask the children to listen with you to a song that's really a prayer to Jesus (explain that "yay-soo" means "Jesus"). Then invite the children to join in singing the chorus as you play the song through once more. If you wish, they can sway gently from side to side or tap the beat lightly on their knees (a simple, two-beat measure).

Follow the song with an art time, during which the children can cut out a paper doll chain. Give each child a sheet of paper and show the group how to fold it, accordian style, like this:

 tip Save time and frustration for younger children by handing them pre-folded papers. Help them draw the figure or do it for them, if necessary. You may even want to pre-cut the figures for little ones and just let them add faces!

Have them draw an outline of a person on the top piece, like this:

Next, supply scissors and have the kids cut out their figures. Older kids can help out younger ones who may have trouble cutting through all the layers of the paper. Show them how to pull the layers apart to make a chain of people.

Invite the children to think of someone they can pray for or help in some other way. They may print that person's name on one of the paper people and/or color it to remind them of that person. If time permits, they can add the name of another person or two on their paper chain. Encourage them to take the chains home and continue to add people to it.

Hands That Care

Option to step 3

Music Smart   Picture Smart   Word Smart   People Smart   Self Smart

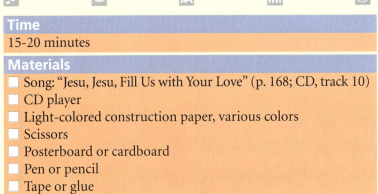

Time
15-20 minutes

Materials
☐ Song: "Jesu, Jesu, Fill Us with Your Love" (p. 168; CD, track 10) ☐ CD player ☐ Light-colored construction paper, various colors ☐ Scissors ☐ Posterboard or cardboard ☐ Pen or pencil ☐ Tape or glue

Note: This idea comes from *Hand in Hand: Helping Children Celebrate Diversity* (Faith Alive Christian Resources, p. 53).

Use this option if you're looking for an art activity that requires somewhat less dexterity than the paper people chain described above. Begin with the time of wondering, then the song. After the song, distribute half sheets of light-colored construction paper to the children. Have them trace and cut out the shape of one of their hands. Ask them to write or draw a picture on the palm and or/fingers of a way or ways they can help others.

Using a wreath-shaped piece of posterboard or cardboard, tape or glue the paper hands into a circle. Display the circle of hands on your wall.

4 SHOW
Unit and Session Projects

Goal
Show Jesus' love to someone in need.
Time
15-30 minutes or more
Materials
See individual projects for lists

Below are a variety of projects to help the children apply this parable to their lives. Some of the projects are continuations from the first session and can run for the entire unit, others are for just this session. Choose one or more that best suits your time frame and the interests and abilities of the children.

Unit Project Ideas

Memory Fun Word Smart

Time
5-10 minutes
Materials
☐ Flashlight

Most of the children in your group will know the Memory Fun verse by today. Turn on the flashlight as you have in previous weeks and invite the whole group to say the verse with you. You might want to ask them to remember some of the stories they heard from God's Word in the past few weeks, stories Jesus told. Remind them that Jesus told those stories to show us how to live, just like shining a flashlight in a dark room helps us walk without stubbing our toes!

Just for fun, you may want to review the memory verse one more time, word by word. Ask the children to form a circle or line. Give the flashlight to the first person. He should say the first word of the verse, then pass the flashlight to the next person in line. She says the second word, then passes the light to the third person in line who says the third word, and so on. Assure the children that if they don't remember a word, they can just pass the light on to the next person. Go through the verse several times this way. Praise your kids for being such good rememberers!

Sharable Parable Bookmarks Picture Smart Word Smart

Time
15-20 minutes
Materials
☐ Bookmark pattern (reproducible page 187)
☐ Crayons
☐ Paper punch
☐ Construction paper circles, various colors
☐ Glue sticks
☐ Small pieces of ribbon

With today's bookmark, the children can complete their set of five. Run copies of the pattern (p. 189) on heavy stock. Younger children can simply color in the circles to make a picture or design that reminds them of the story. Older children can glue on paper-punched circles of various colors of construction for a mosaic look.

For today's session, kids could make an outline of a hand, as a symbol of reaching out and helping others. A heart as a symbol of love (if not used with the previous parable) would also be appropriate. Even a pattern resembling a Band-Aid would do! Again, there's room at the bottom to print a title or Scripture location of the parable. Attach a ribbon through a hole punched at the top of the bookmark.

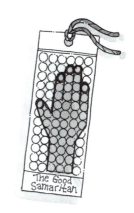

Encourage kids to show the bookmark to their families and friends and to share the parable with them.

Storybooks AA Word Smart   Picture Smart   People Smart

Time
15 minutes

Materials
☐ Storybook, "The Parable of the Good Samaritan" (reproducible pages 213-214), one set per child ☐ Crayons

Each of the five sessions offers a take-home storybook that the children may share with their family and friends. For today's session, photocopy pages 213-214 and distribute a set to each child. Walk the children through the folding process, offering your help and the help of older children to the little ones in your group.

1. Fold both pages in half horizontally along the dotted lines.

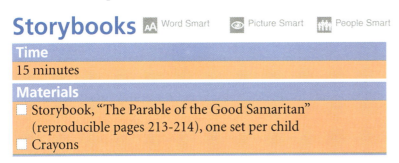

2. Fold both pages in half vertically along the dotted lines.

3. Insert the second set of folded pages into the first set, so that page 3 is opposite page 2.

Have kids print their names on the cover, then color in the pictures. (If short on time, just read the booklet with them, letting them color it at home.) Encourage them to read the story with their family and friends.

One-Session Project Ideas
Action Outing   People Smart   Body Smart   Music Smart   Earth Smart

Time
15 minutes for planning; actual outing time will vary
Materials
Vary according to which project is chosen

How can your children show Jesus' love to someone in need? The following types of projects, while not long or involved, would really help the children apply this parable to their lives:

- Sing at a rest home or at an elderly person's home.
- Bake cookies and bring them to an elderly, homebound person from your congregation.
- Visit your local food pantry or community kitchen and volunteer to help.
- Pick up litter in someone's yard or in a park or other public place (kids can make their own litter bags).
- Collect groceries and deliver food baskets (check with your deacons for recipients).
- Help older kids on a neighborhood clean-up project.
- Help set tables at a church money-raising supper.
- Make cards (see below) and deliver them to someone from the congregation who is ill or homebound.

These are just a few ideas—no doubt you'll think of others that fit your particular situation. If you go on an outing, remember to

- visit the destination ahead of time; make necessary arrangements with those you are visiting.
- plan the trip carefully with the children, making sure they understand its purpose.
- get written permission from parents/guardians.
- arrange for transportation if needed.
- get help supervising the kids (one adult for every five kids is a recommended ratio).
- talk over the experience when it's done.

Making Cards   Picture Smart   People Smart

Time
15-20 minutes
Materials
☐ Cardstock or light-colored construction paper
☐ Old magazines
☐ Scissors
☐ Glue sticks
☐ Bits of felt, ribbon, cut paper, other materials for decorating cards
☐ Markers, colored pencils, crayons

This project is another way of helping someone in need. It follows the lines of the invitations the children may have made in session 3.

Ahead of time, come up with a list of names of persons from your congregation or community who would appreciate encouragement or get-well cards from young children. You can either send multiple cards to one person (more fun for the person on the receiving end!) or send a separate card to several persons. Be sure to tell the children something about the persons they're sending cards to.

Distribute cardstock or light-colored construction paper and the other materials you've brought. Show kids how to fold the cardstock in half (provide help so the younger children can do this neatly). Some may want to cut people figures or lettering from magazines or catalogs; others may prefer to draw their own illustrations or make a torn-paper collage. Be ready to provide help with an appropriate encouragement or get well message.

If you're sending all the cards to one person, consider whether delivering the cards in person is practical. Would the person receiving the cards appreciate this? If so, you may also want to bake some cookies with the kids and bring them along (or ask for help from their families in doing this).

First-Aid Kits

Picture Smart   Body Smart   Word Smart   People Smart   Music Smart

Time
20-30 minutes
Materials
☐ Empty baby wipe containers or sealable bags, one per child
☐ Good Samaritan puppets and story card copied on heavy paper (reproducible pages 215-216), one set per child
☐ Tongue depressors or large craft sticks, six per child
☐ Scissors
☐ Glue
☐ Various first-aid items: Band-Aids, cotton swabs, sample antiseptic cream, small roll of gauze
☐ Red electrical tape (to make a red cross for box or bag)
☐ Stickers (hearts, Bibles, alphabet letters, medical items) for decorating the container
☐ Crayons, colored pencils, markers
☐ Songs: "Jesu, Jesu, Fill Us with Your Love" and "The Good Samaritan" (pp. 168-170; CD, tracks 10-11; optional)
☐ CD player (optional)

Have the children make and fill Good Samaritan first-aid kits like the one you used in step 2 of this session according to the directions below. Kids can make and color the puppets, then use these items to retell the parable to their family and friends.

tip: Young children may well have difficulty cutting the puppets from heavy paper. To save time and frustration, cut out the puppets prior to your session (or have the older children or other helpers assist them during the session itself).

We suggest first making the boxes, then working on its contents. While the children work, you may want to play the two songs suggested for this session (CD, tracks 10-11).

- Start by distributing an empty, small baby-wipe container or a large sealable bag to each child.
- Show them what your finished kit looks like. Help kids cut two pieces of red electrical tape and stick them to the container or bag to form a cross.
- Hand out Band-Aids and stickers to decorate the containers. Kids can use letter stickers (or a permanent marker) to write "My First Aid Kit" (kindergartners and first graders

will need a lot of help with this!) on the box or bag. When finished, the outside of the container should look something like this:

When the kits are decorated, work on the contents. Distribute the reproducible pages with the puppets and story card (pp. 215-216). Have kids color the figures, then cut them out (see tip, above, for children who can't do the cutting). Give each child six tongue depressors and show them how to glue the figures to the sticks to make puppets, like this:

 If you're running out of time, have the children cut out, color, and glue to a stick only the figures of the good Samaritan and the traveler. The other figures can be done later at home.

Have the children put their puppets and story cards into their kits. Then let the children pick up various first-aid items from a table where you have them displayed (or simply hand them out). If there's still time, encourage the children to use their first-aid kits to tell the story to each other.

Snack: M&M Candies Body Smart

Time
2-3 minutes
Materials
☐ Small bags of multi-colored M&Ms or similar candy

While kids work, let them enjoy a small bag of M&Ms or similar candy as a fun reminder that people of all colors are our neighbors. Make sure there are no kids with allergies before serving this snack.

Small Group Session: Grades 4-8

The Good Samaritan

Scripture
Luke 10:25-37

Memory Challenge
Matthew 7:24-27

Focus
Jesus teaches us who our neighbors are and tells us we should love them.

1 HELLO
Breaking Down Barriers

Body Smart · People Smart · Word Smart

Goal
Introduce the idea that the Samaritan broke a barrier to help someone in need.

Time
10 minutes

Materials
☐ Shelf paper or several sheets of newsprint taped together, prepared as described below
☐ Old magazines (optional)
☐ Masking tape

Have the doorway to your room blocked off, using large butcher paper (available from a teacher store) or several sheets of newsprint taped together. Use masking tape to tape the barrier in place. On the paper write words or place pictures cut from magazines that suggest things that keep us from showing love and kindness to each other. Use words and pictures that depict anger, fear, pride, hatred, racism, prejudice, jealousy, violence, social status, and so on.

Be sure to meet the kids at the door (before they break through the paper!). Explain that the parable for today is about a Samaritan who broke a barrier by helping someone in need. He didn't care about the other person's race or social status. Ask kids to look at the words and pictures on the paper barrier and name some of the things that keep people from being good neighbors to others.

Then let the kids break through the barrier into your classroom.

> **time saver** Don't spend a lot of time now on the barriers. We'll revisit them in step 3.
>
> However, if you're willing to have this opening activity take a bit longer, have the group help you find pictures from old magazines and write words on the paper that keep us from helping others. Then tape the barrier to your door and burst through it.

② KNOW
Picturing the Story

Picture Smart, Word Smart, Number Smart

Goal
Explain why Jesus told this story.
Time
20 minutes
Materials
☐ Bibles
☐ One or more sections of paper tablecloth, 6'-8' (2-3 m) long
☐ Markers or crayons, various colors

Begin by distributing Bibles and having everyone find the parable of the good Samaritan in Luke 10:25-37. Ask for volunteers to take turns reading through these verses. Then explain that you'd like the kids to work together to picture the parable.

Unfurl a roll of paper tablecloth that's long enough for everyone in the class to work on simultaneously (use two rolls if your group is too large to accommodate working together on the same mural). Place the paper tablecloth on a table or on the floor.

Have group members use their Bibles to decide who will draw what story scene (for large classes have two or more kids work on one scene). Each scene should have a brief caption. We also suggest a final frame that says what the group thinks Jesus is teaching in this parable. A sample arrangement (reduce the number of pictures if your group is small):
- The traveler walking down the path
- The traveler being attacked by robbers
- The priest walking by
- The Levite walking by
- The Samaritan binding up the traveler's wounds
- The Samaritan leading the traveler on his donkey to the inn
- The Samaritan paying the innkeeper
- The meaning of the parable (written out), perhaps with a picture of Jesus talking to a crowd

 tip Encourage your middle schoolers to act as leaders and help decide who will draw and write a caption for each scene. If you are working with younger children, help them to plan the parts of the mural.

Distribute markers and let the group begin planning and working. Review the finished results together, paying particular attention to the last frame, which gives the meaning of the parable. Kids may say that Jesus was teaching us to be like the good Samaritan—to help others when they are in need. Push them a bit further by looking at the context of the parable. Have them open their Bibles and read Luke 10:25-29 again. Ask questions along these lines:
- **What question did the "expert in the law" ask Jesus?**
- **Jesus answered this question by telling the parable. What would that answer be, do you think?**
- **Remember that the Samaritans and Jews hated each other. But the Samaritan didn't let that stop him. What does this say to us about who we should be willing to help?**

Display the finished mural on your classroom wall or in the foyer for the entire congregation to see.

Option to step 2

Dramatization: Contemporary Parable

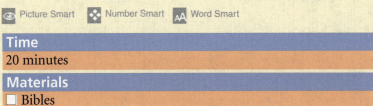
Picture Smart   Number Smart   Word Smart

Time
20 minutes

Materials
☐ Bibles

Use this option if your group enjoys drama and is imaginative. Recasting the story of the good Samaritan in contemporary terms will help your kids to think through the meaning of the parable as they decide who the different characters would be in today's world.

If possible, involve the entire class in presenting one drama (any number of kids can play the robbers). If your class has more than, say, ten kids, you may want to divide into two smaller groups, each preparing and presenting its own drama. Distribute Bibles and have kids find the parable of the good Samaritan (Luke 10:25-37). Ask them to plan and then act out a modern version of the parable. Their modern version can be funny and needn't follow the biblical story exactly; however, they should make the same points as the biblical story.

The group (or groups) should first decide on the details of their modern version of the parable. You may want to jot down questions like these for them to talk about (be ready to provide leadership for discussing these questions if the groups drop the ball):

- Where is our story going to take place? On a lonely street, after dark? On the school playground? In the family car after it's involved in an accident?
- Who will the victim be?
- Who will the good Samaritan be?
- What will be the barrier between the victim and the good Samaritan?
- Who will be the "robbers" that hurt the victim?
- Who will be the priest? The Levite?

Allow about ten minutes for the planning, then jump right into the presentation(s). After the presentation(s), ask, **What is Jesus teaching us in this parable?** See the comments that end step 2 to guide your discussion.

3 GROW
Neighborly Situations

People Smart   Word Smart   Self Smart   Music Smart

Goal
To want to become a true neighbor to more people.

Time
15-20 minutes

Materials
☐ "Neighborly Situations" (reproducible page 217), one copy per person
☐ Song: "Jesu, Jesu, Fill Us with Your Love" (p. 168; CD, track 10)
☐ CD player

This step will help the group recognize some of the barriers that kept the priest and the Levite from helping the wounded person. Begin by asking group members to put themselves in the places of the priest and the Levite and to give excuses for not stopping to help the wounded traveler. Give them a minute to think, then go around the circle and have each person give an excuse that starts with the pronoun "I" (it's OK to repeat an excuse). Offer a couple of sample excuses if kids need help getting started:

- I was just too busy, you know. I had other stuff to do. I didn't have the time to stop.
- I would have helped but I was afraid the robbers might return and beat me up too.
- I thought it was a trap—that the injured man wasn't really injured and would rob me when I got close enough.
- Hey, that guy was a mess! I didn't want to get all dirty trying to help him.
- I thought someone else would come along soon enough and help him.
- I'm too important to go around helping some poor guy in a ditch.
- I don't know—I just didn't feel like it.

Next, focus on excuses we personally give to get out of being a good neighbor. Hand out a copy of "Neighborly Situations" (p. 219) to each person. Read the directions aloud:

Read the role-play situation (below) that you've been asked to do. With one or two partners, act out two different endings: (1) Act out an ending in which you give excuses for not being a good neighbor in this situation. (2) Act out an ending that shows how to be a good neighbor in this situation.

Divide kids into pairs or trios and assign each a role play. There's no need to do all the role plays on the sheet if your group is small or you're running low on time.

After five minutes of planning time, have the partners present their role plays.

 The first three on the sheet can be done with three persons; the remaining situations with two persons. Note that there's a space for those who want to create their own "neighbor" situation (some of your middle schoolers may select this option).

Then remind the group that Jesus told this parable to explain who our neighbors are (everyone!) and how to treat them (with love, as we would want to be treated ourselves). Jesus made the Samaritan, who was hated by the Jews, the hero of the story because Jesus wants us to realize that love for neighbor should not be blocked by race or pride or nationality or any or any other barriers (see list in step 1).

Conclude by asking the group to listen to "Jesu, Jesu, Fill Us with Your Love," a song that's really a prayer to Jesus to show us how to serve our neighbors. Play the song and ask the kids to bow their heads and make it their personal prayer. If your group likes to sing, invite them to join in on the chorus.

Where Am I in This Parable?

Option to step 3

 Self Smart   Music Smart   Word Smart

Time
10 minutes

Materials
☐ "Where Am I in This Parable?" (reproducible page 219), one copy per person
☐ Pen or pencil
☐ Song: "Jesu, Jesu, Fill Us with Your Love" (p. 168; CD, track 10)
☐ CD player

Use this option for a more personal and reflective approach to being a good neighbor. Read the sentence starters to the kids and ask them to take a few minutes to complete two of the statements with their personal thoughts.

Allow five minutes for writing, then invite kids to share any part of their responses that they wish to. Include one of your own responses, if you wish.

Conclude with the comments and the song that end the regular step.

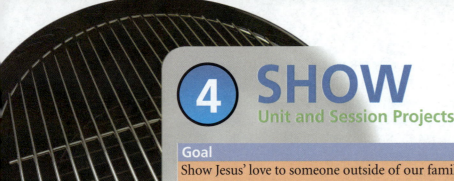

4 SHOW
Unit and Session Projects

Goal
Show Jesus' love to someone outside of our family or immediate social circle.
Time
15-30 minutes or more
Materials
See individual projects for lists

Below are a variety of projects to help group members apply this parable to their lives. Some of the projects are continuations from the first session and can run for the entire unit; others are for just this session. Choose one or more that best suits your time frame and the interests and abilities of your group.

Unit Project Ideas
Memorize and Share a Parable AA Word Smart

Time
5-10 minutes per session
Materials
☐ Memory Challenge (reproducible page 183 or 184)
☐ Chalkboard/chalk or newsprint/markers (optional)

Spend a few minutes today giving the kids the opportunity to recite the parable of the wise and foolish builders. Here are a couple of ways to do that (besides saying it in unison):

- Disappearing verse: Write the entire Memory Challenge on your board or on newsprint. Say it together in unison. Then erase or mark over a word or phrase; again, have the group recite the parable in unison, filling in the missing words. Continue until the entire passage has "disappeared."
- Word cards: Divide the Memory Challenge into short phrases and write these on plain white paper, using markers. Hand the cards out randomly and let group members arrange the cards in the proper sequence.
- Write or recite: Give kids the choice of reciting the verse to a partner or writing it out.

Be sure to commend everyone for learning a parable (including those who may have struggled to learn it correctly). Encourage them to keep on memorizing parts of God's Word.

Sharable Parable Bookmarks 👁 Picture Smart   AA Word Smart

Time
15-20 minutes
Materials
☐ Bookmark pattern (reproducible page 187)
☐ Crayons
☐ Paper punch
☐ Construction paper, various colors
☐ Glue sticks
☐ Small pieces of ribbon

With today's bookmark, group members can complete their set of five. Run copies of the pattern (p. 187) on heavy stock. Kids can make a picture or design that relates to today's parable, either by coloring in circles or gluing on paper-punched circles of various colors of construction paper for a mosaic look.

For today's session, kids could make an outline of a hand as a symbol of reaching out and helping others. A heart as a symbol of love (if not used with previous parables) would also be appropriate. Even a pattern resembling a Band-Aid would do! As with the other bookmarks, there's room at the bottom to print a title or Scripture location of the parable. Attach a ribbon through a hole punched at the top of the bookmark.

Encourage kids to show the bookmark and share the parable with their families and friends.

Sun Art   Picture Smart   Earth Smart

Time
15-20 minutes
Materials
☐ Construction paper, various dark colors
☐ Removable glue sticks (check your local craft store)
☐ Scissors
☐ Toothpicks
☐ Pen

This project, adapted from a Martha Stewart newspaper column, uses the power of the sun to make a unique kind of art. Kids can make interesting illustrations related to the parables they're learning. The basic idea is that cutout shapes are placed on a sheet of colored construction paper. Cut shapes from construction paper and glue with removable glue to the sheet. Then tape the sheet, cutouts facing out, to a window where it will catch a lot of sun. After a week or so (longer if higher contrast is desired), peel off the cutouts. The images will be bold and sharp on the construction paper, while the paper surrounding the images has faded in color.

For today's session on the parable of the good Samaritan, kids could make a heart or a helping hand or use their own (better!) ideas. Letters also can be used as cutouts for those who want to label their artwork.

Kids can take this project home today, hang it in a sunny window, and let the sun do its work for a week or so. They can add this sun print to the others they've already made. Encourage them to show their art to their family and friends and explain how it relates to the parable of the good Samaritan.

125

One-Session Project Ideas

 tip Several of the activities suggested in previous sessions would also work well today, assuming you haven't already used them. Consider adding the following to the choices below:

- Community/Acceptance/Affirmation Circle (session 4, p. 103) provides a way for kids to affirm each other as neighbors.
- A Prayer for Openness (sessions 3 and 4, p. 104) works very well with the themes of the parable of the good Samaritan.
- A Taste of Diversity (session 3, p. 75) would make a fun feast with which to end the unit and serve as a reminder of the diversity of cultures.

Action Outing   People Smart   Body Smart   Picture Smart   Earth Smart

Time
15 minutes for planning; actual outing time will vary

Materials
Vary according to which project is chosen

How can your kids show Jesus' love to someone outside of their family or immediate social circle? Here are a few projects that needn't be long or involved but that would really help the group apply this parable to their lives.

- Give away the bookmarks, sun art, and other projects you've made during this unit to younger children as a gift or to the children's wing of a local hospital.
- Sing at a rest home or at an elderly person's home.
- Bake cookies and bring them to an elderly, homebound person from your congregation.
- Visit your local food pantry or community kitchen and volunteer to help out.
- Clean up someone's yard or a park or other public area.
- Collect groceries and deliver food baskets (check with your deacons for recipients).
- Work at a car wash or church supper to raise funds for helping those in need.
- Make cards (see below) and deliver them to someone from the congregation who is ill or homebound.

These are just a few ideas—no doubt you'll think of others that fit your particular situation. If you go on some kind of outing, remember to

- visit the destination ahead of time and make any necessary arrangements.
- plan the trip carefully with the kids, making sure they understand its purpose.
- get written permission from parents.
- arrange for transportation, if needed.
- get help in supervising the kids (one adult for every five kids is a recommended ratio).
- talk over the experience when it's done.

Putdown Stompout

 Body Smart   Word Smart   People Smart   Self Smart

Time
15-20 minutes

Materials
☐ Balloons, large enough to write several names on
☐ Markers
☐ Newsprint

Note: This activity is adapted from *Group's Best Jr. Hi Meetings,* Vol. 1 (pp. 96-97).

Ask the group to identify "putdowns" they sometimes hear from kids at school or from their friends or parents. Jot these down on your board or on a sheet of newsprint. Pass out balloons and have kids blow them up, then ask them to write (on the balloons) the putdowns they hate the most. They can either write a word or use a symbol or picture.

Ask someone to read the parable of the good Samaritan. Ask, **Who in this parable are we like when we are hurt by the putdowns of others?** (The victim.) **Who are we like if we put others down with our words?** (The robbers—we attack people with our words and we rob them of their pride and dignity.)

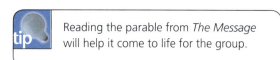

Reading the parable from *The Message* will help it come to life for the group.

Mix up the balloons so that no one knows who wrote what. Have kids pick one balloon and read it aloud. Remind them they are reading a putdown that hurts one of their classmates, one of their neighbors. After the reading, have kids place the balloons at their feet and close their eyes. Lead them in this prayer:

> Dear God, putdowns hurt. And you've just heard what hurts us. Use these balloons as symbols of our hurts. Help us to stamp out putdowns. Help us do good things for our friends and even for those we don't like all that much. Let Jesus be our example for loving others. Amen.

Tell kids to stomp on their balloons as together, with God's help, they stamp out putdowns.

Making Cards   Picture Smart   People Smart

Time
15-20 minutes
Materials
☐ Cardstock or light-colored construction paper
☐ Old magazines
☐ Scissors
☐ Glue sticks
☐ Bits of felt, ribbon, cut paper, other materials for decorating cards
☐ Markers, colored pencils, crayons

This project is another way of meeting the goal of helping someone in need. It follows the lines of the invitations suggested in session 3.

Ahead of time, come up with a list of names of persons from your congregation or community who would appreciate encouragement or get-well cards from young children. You can either send multiple cards to one person (more fun for the person on the receiving end!) or send a separate card to several persons. Be sure to tell the children something about the person they're sending cards to.

Distribute the cardstock or construction paper and the other materials you've brought. Kids can fold the cardstock in half or make their own creative folds. Some may want to cut pictures from magazines; others may prefer to draw their own illustrations or make a torn-paper collage. Let them have fun and be creative and encouraging in the messages they write. A little humor is always appreciated!

If you're sending all the cards to one person, consider whether delivering the cards as a group is practical. Would the person receiving the cards appreciate this? If so, you may also want to bake some cookies with the kids and bring them along (or ask for help from their families in doing this).

First-Aid Kits

👁 Picture Smart   🚶 Body Smart   AA Word Smart   👥 People Smart   🎵 Music Smart

Time
20 minutes

Materials
☐ Empty baby wipe containers or sealable bags, one per person
☐ Good Samaritan puppets and story card copied on heavy paper (reproducible pages 215-216), one set per person
☐ Tongue depressors or large craft sticks, six per child
☐ Scissors
☐ Glue
☐ Various first-aid items: Band-Aids, cotton swabs, sample antiseptic cream, small roll of gauze
☐ Red electrical tape (to make a red cross for box or bag)
☐ Stickers (hearts, Bibles, alphabet letters, medical items) for decorating the container
☐ Crayons, colored pencils, markers
☐ Songs: "Jesu, Jesu, Fill Us with Your Love" and "The Good Samaritan" (pp. 169-171; CD, tracks 10-11; optional)
☐ CD player (optional)

If you do this project, be sure to present it as something your kids can make, then give to younger children as a gift. Another possibility is to give the kits to the children's wing of a local hospital. Still another is to have your kids help children in grades K-3 make their own kits. (Leaders of young children will welcome some help with this project!)

We suggest first making the boxes, then working on its contents. While the kids are working, you may want to play the two songs suggested for this session (CD, tracks 10-11).

- Start by distributing an empty, small baby-wipe container or a large sealable bag to each child.
- Show them what your finished kit looks like. Help kids cut two pieces of red electrical tape and stick them to the container or bag to form a cross.
- Hand out Band-Aids and stickers to decorate the containers. Kids can use letter stickers (or a permanent marker) to write "My First Aid Kit" on the box or bag. When finished, the outside of the container should look something like this:

When the kits are decorated, work on the contents. Distribute the reproducible pages with the puppets and story card (pp. 215-216). Have kids color the figures and cut them out. Have kids glue the figures to tongue depressors to make puppets, like this:

Have kids put the puppets and story cards into their kits. Then have them choose various first-aid items from your supply. If you're going to give the kits to younger children or to a local hospital, collect them now and be sure to tell kids where the boxes are headed. Otherwise send them home with your kids and encourage them to give them to a younger child from their neighborhood.

Snack: M&M Candies Body Smart

Time
2-3 minutes
Materials
☐ Small bags of multi-colored M&Ms or similar candy

While kids work, let them enjoy a small bag of M&Ms or similar candy as a fun reminder that people of all colors are our neighbors. Make sure there are no kids with allergies before serving this snack.

The Sower and the Seeds
Based on Matthew 13:3-8, 18-23

Characters (in order of appearance)
Farmer
Bird
Rock
Thorn
Road Seed
Burned Seed
Choked Seed
Good Seed

Suggested Costumes
Farmer: jeans, straw hat, sack for seed
Bird: beak made from cardboard, darkened with marker, attached with elastic to actor's head
Rock: gray clothing (or plain clothing with construction paper rocks pinned on)
Thorn: tan clothes with actor carrying a bunch of twigs or brambles
Road Seed: tan clothes (these seeds are eaten before they have a chance to grow)
Burned Seed: green clothes with swatches of red felt to represent being burned by the sun
Choked Seed: green clothes with a necktie around neck to represent choking
Good Seed: green clothes

Props
Brown sheets to cover up all seeds
Rocks to pile around Rock
Small branches to pile around Thorn
Sacajawea coin (U.S. dollar coin; optional)

Setting/Synopsis
Farmer enters, scattering imaginary seeds. He meets three characters—Bird, Rock, and Thorn—who are questioning and mocking him because he is planting. Bird intends to eat all the seeds. Rock is sitting in the middle of a pile of rocks. Thorn is standing straight as an arrow. Farmer meets them one at a time as he comes sowing his seeds.

Near Bird, Rock, and Thorn are lumps on the ground covered over with brown sheets. These are the main seed characters—Road Seed, Burned Seed, Choked Seed—dressed as described above. There are many other lumps scattered around too. These are all the characters playing the Good Seeds that will survive and grow.

Farmer speaks with Bird, Rock, and Thorn. Then the respective seeds that fall near these characters begin to grow. Road Seed doesn't get very far before being eaten. Burned Seed grows up but overheats and dies. Choked Seed gets all choked up with money worries. Finally, all the Good Seeds come to life in two waves, proving what the Farmer has contended all along—the harvest will happen.

Farmer: *[enters and begins sowing]* Hi. I'm the farmer. I'm going to sow some seeds in my kingdom. "Sowing" just means I'm going to plant some seeds. I'm going to scatter seeds near and far. Hither and yon. Far and wide. *[smiling]* Let's see what happens as I do that, shall we?

Bird: You think you're so smart scattering those seeds, Mr. Farmer. Well, I've got news for you—I've got a lot of cousins, and we all *love* to eat seeds. You just keep throwing those nice seeds down, and we'll just keep gobbling them up. Ha, ha, ha! You really think your seeds are going to grow? Hah! Not while I'm around.

Farmer: Oh, I'm not worried, Mr. Bird. I've got more seeds than you and your friends could eat in a lifetime. These seeds *will* grow and you're not going to believe your eyes. Because once they start growing, there will be a tremendous harvest. You'll see.

Bird: Whatever you say, Mr. Farmer. My, these seeds are deeeeelicious. *[pretends to eat a bunch]* MmmMmm. Good. Heh, heh, heh, heh, heh.

Farmer: *[continues scattering]* Some seed over here and some seed there.

Rock: *[some land on Rock]* Hey, watch it! What do you think you're doing?

Farmer: Why, planting seeds, of course. What's wrong?

Rock: Can't you see this is a rock garden? Nothing grows by a pile of rocks. Soil's not deep enough here. Everybody knows seeds don't grow in shallow, rocky soil. *[mocking]* You call yourself a farmer. What kind of farmer are you?

Farmer: I'm a farmer who likes to plant lots and lots of seeds. Wherever I go, I plant seeds. This land here is my kingdom. And I love to watch seeds grow. Of course I know there are places where they won't grow. But I have so many seeds to plant that some are bound to grow somewhere in my kingdom. You'll see. Someday there will be all kinds of plants around here. Even near the rocks. You'll see. Trust me. It's my kingdom.

Rock: I'll be watching all right. But I still think you really don't know what you're doing.

Farmer: Trust me, I know what I'm doing. Pretty soon, there will be all kinds of nice green plants around here. *[gestures around as if there's not a person anywhere for miles]* Everyone will be talking about it.

Rock: *Who's* going to be talking about it?

Farmer: Why, the plants of course.

Rock: *[sarcastically]* The plants that aren't here yet?

Farmer: Exactly. You catch on pretty fast.

Rock: You know what they say: A rolling stone gathers no moss. And I'm pretty quick.

Farmer: That you are. Just be careful not to get stuck between a rock and a hard . . . well, never mind. I've got to keep planting. Some over here and some over there.

Thorn: Say, Mr. Farmer.

Farmer: Hello, Mr. Thorn.

Thorn: Don't tell me you're planting seeds again! When are you going to give up?

Farmer: Oh, I don't give up too easily.

Thorn: Yes, but look at me. I'm a thorn and you're scattering seeds right near me. Those poor little seeds will never, never grow. I'll choke them to death! *[makes choking motion with hands]* Ha, ha!

Farmer: You're wrong, Mr. Thorn. They *will* grow. And they will bear tons of delicious fruit! Just trust me. In my kingdom, there will be many blessings and good things for all the seeds that grow. And those seeds will be a blessing to others. The harvest is coming, Mr. Thorn.

Thorn: Uh, I don't think so, Mr. Farmer. We thorns are just too mean and nasty to let your seeds grow.

Farmer: You will see some coming up real soon. *[turns back toward where Bird was]* In fact, I think I see a seed about to sprout up right now!

[Road Seed lifts head—but nothing more—from under brown sheet; then sings or says the following (for music, see p. 135; CD, track 3)]

Road Seed: I am a little seed, this message you must heed.
You don't need Weed 'n Feed to stay a seed indeed.
I heard about his kingdom, and I really don't get it.
But does it even matter? I'd rather not be in it.

[Bird begins to make his way over to Road Seed.]

Look! Here comes a bird. He's coming right at me.
Oh, no, I think he's eating—at least that's what I see.
He's eating little seeds, I think he's having lunch.
I think I'm next to go snap, crackle, pop, and crunch.

[At the word crunch *Bird aims beak down to eat seed, then pulls the brown sheet back over Road Seed's head. Bird then looks up at Farmer and says the following in a singsong, mocking tone.]*

Bird: So sorry, Mr. Farmer, but I really am starved. And like I said before, you're not going to harvest *anything* this year.

Farmer: Be patient. Look—another seed is sprouting!

[Burned Seed comes to life from under brown sheet and sprouts up yawning and stretching the whole way. Then says the following line with arms (branches) up in the air]

Burned Seed: Oh, it's great to be a plant at last! And the weather is so beautiful outside. It's even hot. Whew! *[pauses for a second, then realizes it's going to be way too hot, getting nervous]* It's like an oven out here. It's way too hot! My roots just aren't deep enough. Oh, oh. Overheating. Dehydrating. Heat Stroke. Sun Stroke. Withering. *[collapses and pulls sheet back over]*

Rock: Well, that poor little seed didn't last long, Mr. Farmer. This is no place to plant seeds, I tell you.

Farmer: Just wait a little longer, and you'll see. Why don't you trust me? Here comes another seed popping up.

[Choked Seed comes to life from under brown sheet and sprouts up, yawning and stretching the whole way. Then sings or says the following line with arms up in the air, hamming it up. This seed is about to get choked by money worries. (CD, track 4. Song is loosely based on the Veggie Tales "Bunny" song from Rack, Shack, and Benny: A Lesson in Handling Peer Pressure.*)]*

Choked Seed: Well, Jesus told me 'bout blessings so nice,
he's got kingdom riches of incredible price.
Bless me now, don't wait, my things accumulate.
I'll take it all with me through heaven's gate.

I like to hoard my money and hide my wealth.
I like to keep it all, keep it all for myself.
This crazy conversation 'bout bearing fruit,
It's startin' to worry me—I want to stockpile my loot!

So let me keep my cash, can't bear to let it go.
Don't make me give it away, tho' that's the way to grow.
I'm just a choked up seed, with lots of seed money.
Be fruitful God says—I think that's really funny.

So I think I'll stay greedy, without bearing fruit. *[hold up Sacajawea coin]*
It's overrated, you know, and Sacajawea's so cute.
Without my money I sit on needles and pins.
My motto's always been, the one with the most toys wins.

The money, the money, ooooh I love the money!
I don't want fruit, won't you show me the money?
The money, the money, ooooh I'm so torn.
I'll take the money—even if, in my side, it's a thorn.

[smiles and pauses briefly, looking fondly at the Sacajawea coin]

Oh, I love that money song. But I just get all choked up when I talk about money. I start worrying about not having enough. And then I get *[begins to cough]* all choked up. *[coughs loudly again]* Oh, those miserable thorns. *[holds throat]* I'm all choked up. I'm a goner.

[Choked Seed collapses and pulls sheet over himself.]

Thorn: I hate to say I told you so, Mr. Farmer. But I told you so!

Rock: We all told you.

Bird: That's right. You told us to be patient, but now look what has happened. Some of your seeds got eaten by the birds. Some landed in shallow soil among the rocks, and when the sun came up, the plants quickly died. And the thorns choked out a whole bunch of your other seeds. Your kingdom sure doesn't have much of a harvest, Mr. Farmer.

Farmer: I told you to wait, Mr. Thorn, Mr. Rock, and Mr. Bird. And now the time has come. Watch!

[Suddenly, a first wave of green plants comes to life from under their brown sheets. They yawn, stretch out, and wave their arms.]

Thorn: I can't believe my eyes! Do you see all those beautiful green plants!

Rock: Wow!

Bird: Chirp! Chirp!

Farmer: Just keep watching. There's more on the way *[second wave of seeds comes to life from under brown sheets]*. These plants will spread the word and more seeds will grow. And then more and then more. Until my kingdom is filled to overflowing. Until my kingdom garden is complete! Do you trust me now?

Thorn: Spectacular!

Rock: Fantastic!

Bird: Wow!

Farmer: That's right, and that's my kingdom!

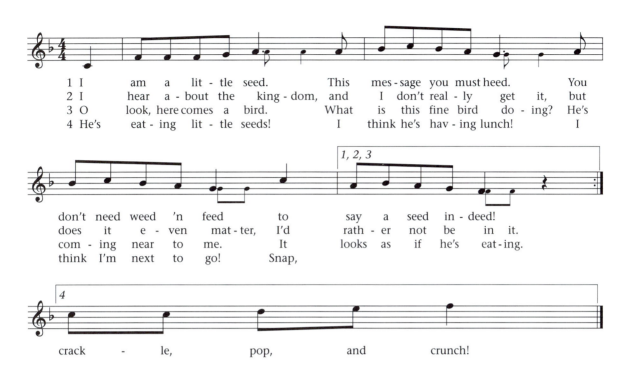

The Wise and Foolish Builders
Based on Matthew 7:24-27

Characters (in order of appearance)
Director (Offstage voice)
Rob Selah (Host of *This New House*)
Rocky Mountain (Owner of Rocky Mountain Builders)
Iron Ore (Bricklayer for Rocky Mountain Builders)
Granite (Bricklayer for Rocky Mountain Builders)
Sandy (Owner of Sandland Builders; contemporary surfer dude or dudette)
Shoreline (Worker for Sandland Builders; contemporary surfer dude or dudette)

Note: Rob Selah's last name comes from the musical term used in the psalms that encourages readers to pause and reflect. *Selah* also rhymes with *Vila,* as in Bob Vila who began the barrage of home improvement shows on television with the series *This Old House.*

Sandy and Shoreline are meant to be California surfer types with their accompanying jargon and peculiar way of speaking. These particular surfers/builders do have not a lot of smarts. The actors are supposed to emphasize this and ham it up.

Suggested Costumes
Rob Selah: jeans, a flannel shirt, a plastic hard hat, and a tool belt

Rocky Mountain, Iron Ore, and Granite: jeans and plastic hard hats; carry trowels, hammers, screwdrivers, and so on

Sandy and Shoreline: Anything casual and beachy, carry sand pails and sand shovels.

Props and Set
Divide the stage into two areas: Rocky Mountain Builders and Sandland Builders. The Rocky Mountain site can feature large rocks, bricks, trowels, hammers, saws, screwdrivers, and other actual tools. The Sandland site can feature a couple of surfboards, bags of sand, shovels, sandpails, a kiddie pool, and so on.

Have "The Wise Man and the Foolish Man" (theme music) ready to go on your CD player (track 6) or play it live.

Setting/Synopsis
The TV show *This New House* is about to begin. Two building companies are on stage at their respective building sites, pretending to build foundations. For the Sandland Company builders, this means they are playing in the sand. Theme music begins as the Director starts the countdown to the show, and the music fades out as lines begin. Rob Selah begins explaining today's show, then interviews the two companies who are building foundations for new homes. Selah points out the some big differences in the building materials and how the builders build, then suggests that only one group has it right. Theme music begins again as actors exit.

Director: And we are live in 7 . . . 6 . . . cue music *[theme music starts playing]* . . . 4 . . . 3 . . . 2 . . . 1 . . . You're live, Rob.

Selah: Good day, ladies and gentlemen, boys and girls, and welcome to *This New House.* I'm Rob Selah, your host, and have we got an important show for you today! Today we're going to learn about foundations. Foundations are what houses get built on. And that's pretty important way out here on the California coast. We're going to interview two different builders today to show you two different types of foundations. So let's get started. First stop—Rocky Mountain Builders. And this is Mr. Rocky Mountain himself. Hello there, Mr. Mountain.

Rocky: Please call me Rocky, OK? And say hello to my helpers, Iron Ore and Granite.

Selah: Hello there, Iron Ore. Granite. *[shakes hands]* Well, I've got one big question for you today, and here it is: What's the best material to build your house on? Wood? Gravel? Sticks? Clay?

Iron Ore: Actually, none of the above, Mr. Selah. *[pause]* Now granted . . . *[immediately interrupted by Granite]*

Granite: What do you want, Iron Ore?

Iron Ore: What do you mean, "What do I want?" *[immediately understands that Granite misunderstood him]* Oohh, I said "granted,"—not Granite. Now granted, we could have chosen those other building materials . . . *[interrupted by Granite]*

Granite: Yeah, we could have used something Iron Ore. Get it? Iron Ore?

Iron Ore: *[rolling eyes]* Yeah, good one Granite. Iron Ore, that's my name. Ha, ha. But can we get on with the show here? As I was saying, we could have used those other materials, but ol' Rocky here had something else in mind. And Rocky's the boss.

Selah: I bet I can guess. You're using some of that newfangled concrete then, is that it?

Granite: Wrong again, Mr. Selah.

Selah: Well then, what did you use? Tell us, you're the experts.

Iron Ore: Sure thing, Rob. The absolute best way to build your house . . .

Granite: The absolute best thing to build your house on . . .

Rocky: The absolute best foundation for a house is-s-s-s-s *[elongates the word]* rock. That's right, rock. Just like my name—Rocky. We always build our houses on rock.

Iron Ore: Yep, it's gotta be rock. Nothing else will do. Rock it is. Has to be. I mean, rock even blunts scissors, you know. As long as you have rock underneath your house, your foundation is strong, and your house is going to last and last and last. Gotta be rock, I always say. Because rock is strong.

Selah: Well, I'll grant you that, Iron Ore.

Granite: What? *[to Selah]* Did you call me?

Selah: No! *[somewhat amused by Granite's inability to distinguish between granted and Granite.]* I was just agreeing with Iron Ore that a foundation made of rock looks strong. Real strong. I'll bet your house can weather just about any storm.

Rocky: You better believe it. *[thoughtfully]* You know what it's like? It's kinda like reading your Bible and doing what it says; obeying the Word of God. If you do that, God will make you nice and strong. Give you strength. He will grant it.

Granite: What? Did you call me, Boss?

All characters *[in unison]* No! No! No! *[now they are all exasperated at Granite]*

Rocky: Anyway, rock's the only way to go. But I think a storm is coming, so we've gotta keep working. Thanks for the publicity, Mr. Selah. *[looks at pretend camera to plug his company]*

Remember, all of you out there in TV land, just call Rocky Mountain Builders for houses that last and last and last.

Selah: Thank you, Rocky. Get that work finished now. *[moving over to next site]* Well, onto another builder over here. It looks like a, uh, *[not too impressed and showing it through facial expression and tone of voice]* totally different foundation here. Hello there, sir.

Sandy: Dude, call me Sandy. My company is Sandland Builders. And now say hello to my best building bud: Shoreline.

Selah: Hello, Short Line. *[Selah pronounces it wrong]*

Shoreline: Way cool. You just called me a railroad, dude. Not SHORTline. SHOREline. Shoreline. As in beach. As in coast. As in waves and hangin' 10. As in ocean-front property. Get it, dude?

Selah: Sorry, Shoreline. My mistake.

Shoreline: No problemo! *[pronounced "pro-blame-oh"]*

Selah: Sandy, tell me, what do you build your houses on? *[skeptical]* You do build houses, don't you?

Sandy: Oh yeah, our houses are fly, dude. And we use the best stuff. Hang loose a second. I'll get you a sample of our building material. *[digs in bag of sand]* Here you go, dude. Or do you prefer dudesicle?

Selah: Actually, Rob would be fine, thanks.

Sandy: Rob it is. Glad you didn't say "Selah." Now that's a weird name, dude.

Selah: *[bewildered, yet hoping]* So I assume you do use this sand to make concrete. Am I right?

Shoreline: Rob dude, do we look that stupid?

Sandy: Yeah, like we just came over on our surfboards from uh, the Netherlands? You think because we're so buff *[both pose their muscles for a second, like they are in a Mr. Universe contest]* we don't know anything? Because we can hang-10 with our eyes closed, we don't know how to build houses? Give us some credit, dude. Everybody knows you can't make concrete out of sand.

Selah: *[feeling reprimanded]* All right, all right. So what *do* you build your houses on?

Shoreline: Rob dude . . . *[thinks Selah is being deliberately slow to understand]* You're holding it in your hand! It's the sand, the sand!

Selah: Sand . . . the sand? *[in disbelief]*

Sandy: *[glances around in amazement]* Wooaaahhh!! Did you hear that echo, Shoreline? Yeah, the sand, dude.

Selah: *[laughing uproariously]* Shoreline, what happens when the storm comes, when the rain beats down, when the ocean waves blast in, when the wind really blows and beats against the house? Won't it come crashing down? Or at least get awfully lopsided? What about El Niño?

Sandy: El Who-oh?

Selah: Oh, never mind. But don't your houses fall down a lot?

Shoreline: Sure they do, dude, but not to worry. Sand is everywhere and sand is cheap. If the house falls down, we'll just rebuild it. You know, like, start all over, from scratch?

Sandy: It's really no big deal. Last year, we built 40 houses and 37 of them fell splat during one huge storm. But oh man, you should have seen the monster surf that day.

Selah: So did those 37 people—the ones whose houses fell flat in the storm—did they call you to rebuild?

Shoreline: Uh, uh, hmmm . . . *[scratching head]* Can't say they did, Rob dude. . . . Come to think of it, no one called. Wonder why?

Selah: May I suggest something?

Sandy: Sure, Mr. Selah dude. Anything. Go ahead.

Selah: Maybe you should start building your houses on the rock. And you know what else? God says that about your lives too. That you should build on the rock of the Bible—and do what it says.

Sandy: Well, that's something to think about, I guess. But right now, surf's up. Storm's coming. Gotta go. Later.

Shoreline: Me too. See ya. Hang loose, dude.

Selah: *[moves away from the builders for his final comments]* Well, that's our report. *[with concern]* Two very different builders. Rocky and his helpers building their houses and their lives on the Rock and on the Bible, obeying Jesus, doing what he says. And Sandy and Shoreline building on the sand. Seems to me that Sandy and Shoreline are heading for disaster when that storm hits. And Rocky, Iron Ore, and Granite—well, I think they'll make it through OK. If you ask me, we've got one group of wise builders and one group of foolish builders. *[theme music begins, plays until drama ends]* So until next time, this is Rob Selah for *This New House*. *[music gets louder as actors exit stage.]*

The Great Banquet
Based on Luke 14:16-24

Characters (in order of appearance)
Rehoboam (Reporter, something of a cross between a reality TV show and a Hollywood gossip columnist)
Banquet (Wealthy man who is preparing and throwing a huge banquet)
Seriah (Banquet's secretary)
Festus (Wealthy real estate developer)
Orpah (Wealthy cattle rancher)
Markus (Wealthy, newly married)

Suggested Costumes
Characters can wear either modern-day clothing or first-century costumes (bathrobes, sandals, head-wrap, and so on).

Set and Props
The set is simple—just a table in the background set for dinner to suggest the banquet hall. Chairs around the table. Or leave the stage empty, with the audience simply assuming the banquet table is off-stage, perhaps through a set of exit doors. You'll also need stage space for the encounters between Seriah and those who are invited to the banquet.

Additional props:

- Rehoboam: microphone and clipboard
- Seriah: Palm Pilot (if modern setting); writing tablet or equivalent (if first century)
- Festus: map or set of blueprints that show dimensions of his new property (field)
- Orpah: five-gallon bucket with "FEED" printed on side
- Markus: box of chocolates

Setting/Synopsis
Rehoboam introduces himself (holding cordless microphone) on the air and tells us about the story he is covering. He then becomes a "fly on the wall," watching and occasionally breaking into the story to offer comment. He expresses shock at the scandal that is unfolding before his eyes, yet is happy to get the scoop on the tabloid gossip. Rehoboam stays detached from the story (he doesn't interact with the other characters) until the very end, when Mr. Banquet acknowledges him and draws him into the dialogue. Until that time, however, Rehoboam hovers wherever the action is (sometimes hiding and sneakily listening, other times hamming this up by leaning his ear into a conversation or cupping his hand to his ear). But he must not do so much of this that he draws attention away from the dialogue. During Rehoboam's lines, of course, he pretends that he is in front of the camera giving his commentary. The drama ends with Mr. Banquet and Rehoboam entering the banquet room together, pantomiming talking together and leaving arm-in-arm. Seriah then exits another way to find more banquet attenders.

Rehoboam: *[to camera and audience]* This is Rehoboam—your roving reporter. I'm here covering the story of the century . . . well, actually, it's the banquet of the century. We're covering this story live, in real time, so you won't miss a single moment. No editing. No coaching. Just sheer, raw, real-life, live action, OK? *[pauses briefly, looks down at notes on clipboard]* Now let me give you some background on this breaking story. Word of this mother-of-all-banquets got out several weeks ago, when invitations were sent out to the really important people in town—you know, the society folks, the movers and shakers. Though we tried, we never found out the exact day of the banquet. We've been camped here day and night, watching for the sign that everything is ready. And now . . . *[looks behind him toward the banquet table or into the imaginary banquet hall]* . . . it looks like that's exactly what's going to happen! Here comes Mr. Banquet now—and, oh yes, there's Seriah, his secretary. Let's listen in.

Banquet: *[waving his arm in the direction of the banquet hall]* Well, Seriah, at last everything is ready for my banquet. The finest food is being cooked to perfection right now; the finest wine in the country is ready for all my friends and guests to enjoy. The servers are waiting in the wings, and the entertainers are eager to delight my guests with music.

Seriah: Your guests will all be honored to attend your feast, sir, I'm sure.

Banquet: I certainly hope so. I've spared no expense. All is ready. Now won't you please find all those we invited and tell them to come?

Seriah: As you wish, Mr. Banquet.

Rehoboam: *[breaking in as Seriah leaves Mr. Banquet to find first invitee]* And we're going to follow Seriah as he calls on the rich and famous. Let's go!

[Each of these "chance" encounters with Seriah and the invitees are planned, of course; be creative with your worship space as to how the encounters will happen.]

Seriah: Mr. Festus. I wish to inform you that Mr. Banquet's banquet is now ready for you to enjoy. Please come now—the food and wine are waiting.

Festus: Well . . . I . . . uh . . . um . . . er . . . there's a little problem. See, *[holds up map]* I just bought myself a field. It's right here on the map. And I have to get over there right way and take a look at my property. Please excuse me and give my regrets to Mr Banquet. Maybe next time. . . .

[Seriah is surprised as Festus walks off. Rehoboam takes this opportunity to break in with some comments.]

Rehoboam: *[amazed]* Did you see that? A flat-out refusal to come to the greatest banquet of the century. I wouldn't have believed it if I hadn't seen it with my own eyes. Festus the field-checker. Oh oh oh . . . is he going to miss out, or what? But look! Seriah has found another invitee. Let's tag along.

Seriah: Ms. Orpah. I have the honor of informing you that Mr. Banquet's banquet is now ready. Please come now. The food and wine are waiting.

Orpah: Hmmm. Banquet, you say? Oh right, the invitation of a few weeks ago. I forgot about that. Well . . . *[thinks about her schedule, then holds up feed bucket]* . . . today's not going to work. I just bought some oxen, and I have to feed them you know. In fact, I bought five yoke and that's no joke. *[haughtily]* But then I wouldn't expect you—a humble servant—to understand what kind of money you need to purchase five teams of oxen. Sorry. Can't be there. Have to feed my new purchase. Please excuse me. *[exits]*

Rehoboam: *[breaking in again]* What's this? *Another* refusal? Orpah the oxen-checker this time. Oh my, this *is* getting embarrassing. It will make a great story for tomorrow's tabloids. What if *no one* wants to come to the party? Wouldn't *that* be a story! But wait! It seems that Seriah has found another invitee. Maybe this one will be eager to come.

Seriah: Good day, Mr. Markus. I have been sent to inform you that Mr. Banquet's banquet is now ready. Please come now. The food and wine are waiting.

Markus: Now? Not now! *[laughing]* I just got married. See? *[holds up box of chocolates]* Chocolate! You can't expect a newly married man to go out to a banquet. Especially when he's supposed to be bringing home a box of chocolates for his wife. Nope. I'm taking my year off, just like the law of Moses says I'm entitled to do. Sorry. Please excuse me. Maybe next year . . . *[exits]*

Rehoboam: *[dripping with gossipy compassion]* Oh dear. Markus the married man. This is scandalous. Getting people to come to Mr. Banquet's banquet is proving to be no picnic. All these people, and no one wants to come. But wait! I think Seriah's going to report the bad news to Mr. Banquet himself.

Seriah: Mr. Banquet, sir, I have found all the people you invited to your feast. I'm truly sorry to say that every last one of them declined your invitation. They all had excuses, you see. One had to check out a field he just bought. Another had to feed five teams of expensive oxen she just purchased. And another just got married and wanted to take the year off to be with his wife. These and all the other guests you invited said, "Please excuse me from the banquet." No one is coming, it seems.

Banquet: *[angry]* What! Not coming? All right! They had their chance! *[changing immediately from stern anger to hopeful excitement]* Seriah, I've got an idea! Walk quickly through the town. Invite everyone you see. Everyone, you understand? I don't care if they are rich or poor. I don't care if they are healthy or sick. I don't care if they can see or if they're blind. I don't care if they can walk or if they can't. Bring them in, Seriah.

Seriah: Yes! That's a wonderful idea! *[moves around the stage, as if inviting many people to come to the banquet; returns]* Sir, I've done what you told me to do. But there is still room at the banquet.

Banquet: *[excited, almost happy]* Really? Wonderful! If there is room, more shall come. Seriah, go out once more. This time don't stop at the town. Go out to country roads. Invite whoever you can find. I don't care what they look like, how they speak, what clothes they wear. Bring them all in. Make them come, if you have to. Don't stop until my banquet hall is full.

Seriah: I won't, I promise! *steps to one side as if to leave]*

[Rehoboam just has to reveal himself. He is absolutely amazed at Mr. Banquet.]

Rehoboam: Huhhh? You're going to invite *anyone*?

Banquet: *[turns toward Rehoboam, recognizes him]* I sure am, Rehoboam. Would *you* like to come to my banquet?

Rehoboam: Would I?! But I'm not rich or famous or special. I'm really just a nobody.

Banquet: Not to me, Rehoboam. I'd like you to come to my banquet.

Rehoboam: I'd love to come, but . . . but . . . how do you know my name?

Banquet: *[begins to walk with Rehoboam into banquet hall, but looks back]* Seriah, find them quickly. Fill up my banquet room.

Seriah: Sir, it will be done.

Banquet: Godspeed, Seriah.

Seriah: Thank you, sir. *[all exit]*

The Lost Son
Based on Luke 15:11-22

Characters (in order of appearance)
Dad (Wealthy landowner, loving father of two sons)
Pedro (Older son, loyal to dad and family, hard-working, stay-at-home-type)
Perez (Younger son, rebellious, sick of working, fun-loving, wild)
Narrator (Behind the scenes, invisible to audience)
Penelope Porkman (Wealthy owner of pig farm)
Iheara Pig (Talking pig—name is pronounced "eye-hear-uh")
Phoebe (Maid in dad's household)

Suggested Costumes
Dad and Pedro: similar-looking business suits or other "dressy" clothes
Perez: scruffy jeans, T-shirt, untied shoes, cap on backward, earring, necklace, and so on
Penelope: tidy bib overalls, straw hat, cowboy boots
Iheara Pig: pink snout made of cardboard and attached to head with elastic; brown clothes or burlap wrapping, a tail, and so on
Phoebe: maid uniform

Set and Props
The action takes place in three areas: (1) center stage, where Dad sits behind a desk; (2) aisles, which represent the path home; (3) pigsty, right or left stage, marked by a section of fence. "Fence" can be just a couple of 2 x 4s propped up to suggest a fence.

Additional props:
- five-gallon pail holding some banana chips to feed the pig
- suitcase with some play money sticking out
- stick with a hobo's satchel attached to it
- ring and robe

Setting/Synopsis
Two brothers enter the stage from the side, arguing loudly. As the argument ends, younger brother comes to center stage, older brother exits. Younger brother requests his portion of the estate from Dad. Dad agrees and younger brother takes off (up a church aisle) to spend his fortune. Soon younger brother winds up broke and jobless and gets work from a manager who needs a pig-hand on her farm (stage right or left). Younger brother takes the job; soon "loses it" to the extent that he has a conversation with a pig. He returns to his senses and goes home (racing up and down the aisles) to his dad, who runs out to meet him, embraces him, and forgives him. The celebration begins, but the older brother is angry. Dad talks to him and urges him to forgive.

Pedro: *[heatedly arguing with Perez]* . . . and another thing, little brother—you never lift a finger to help out around here. You just don't do your share, Perez.

Perez: What?! Just because you're a 24-7, holier-than-thou stuffed shirt doesn't mean I don't do anything.

Pedro: OK, little brother. Name me one—just one—project you finished this summer.

Perez: Well, I . . . uh . . . I took the garbage out.

Pedro: Ooohhh. Wow! How long did that take . . . five whole minutes?

Perez: I've had it. You don't think I do my share? Well, I'm outta here! As in gone for good, big brother. As in leaving home. I'm gonna tell Dad right now. *[begins walking to Dad, center stage]*

Pedro: Good! And don't hurry home once your money runs out, you hear? *[exits]*

Perez: Dad, Dad. *[Dad has been sitting at his desk, center stage]* I just can't live here anymore. I'm sick of all the rules. I'm sick of working. I'm sick of my brother. I've just gotta leave. Go someplace far away from here.

Dad: Leave? You mean leave home? For good?

Perez: Yeah, Dad. You get the picture.

Dad: *[sadly]* I'm truly sorry to hear that, son.

Perez: *[lightly, not sensing how his father feels]* Oh, by the way, I'll need the loot I've got coming to me. You know, all the money I'm supposed to get from you when you're dead and gone. My inheritance. I don't want to wait around for it until you're toast. I want it now!

Dad: *[sighs deeply]* Very well. Maybe you're old enough now to make your own decisions. I'll give you your share of our estate and you may go. *[retrieves large suitcase nearby and sets it down by Perez]*

Perez: Oh Dad, that's great! What a relief! *[pauses as he finally sees this is not easy for Dad]* Don't get me wrong—I mean, I like you and everything, but I'm just going crazy with all these other things.

Dad: Say no more, son. I will miss you. Goodbye. *[moves to embrace Perez, who turns away without hugging him]*

Perez: So long, Dad. *[mutters an aside]* So long, work! So long, nasty older brother! Hello, fun and games! *[grabs suitcase with money sticking out and wanders off down aisle, whistling a happy tune; Dad stays at desk; after Perez exits, Narrator gives an update offstage]*

Narrator: Well, folks, I know you'll be disappointed, but we're not going to show you all the wild times Perez had in the far country. Six months have gone by since little brother packed his bags—six long months for Dad and the family back home, but for Perez, it seems like six days. He's got a bunch of wild friends, I hear. Kind of makes me wonder how his money's holding out . . . *[pauses]* Wait a minute! I think I see him coming down the road now. . . . He looks kind of beat, to tell you the truth. Really ragged and ratty. Kinda looks like his money has flown the coop, if you know what I mean.

[Perez enters up the aisle again. This time his suitcase is open and empty; he is devastated, practically crying out his lines.]

Perez: Oh no, can it be true? *[holds up empty suitcase to show audience]* I'm flat broke. But I had tons of money. I couldn't have wasted it all, could I? What was I thinking? Now I'm dying for something to eat—haven't had any real food for days. And all my so-called friends have left me now that my money's gone. I've got to do something to get some money or I'm toast. *[pauses, thinks about what he just said]* Oh man, what I wouldn't give for a nice slice of toast . . . with strawberry jam . . . right now!

[Perez enters the stage, collapses onto his knees near Penelope Porkman, who has entered and is standing near the pigsty.]

Porkman: Well, well—would you look at what the cat dragged in? Another beggar looking for work, just like the rest of them, I suppose. *[gives Perez a nudge with her boot]* Ain't that right, honey?

Perez: Huh? What? Who are you? Am I dreaming?

Porkman: Nope, you're not dreaming, sugar. My name's Penelope Porkman, and I've got work for you, if you want to do it. I've got pigs. I've got horses. I've got chickens. I've got cows—and they all need to be fed, city boy. It's hard, dirty work, especially the pigs. My, oh my, how they do smell.

Perez: *[sheepishly]* I'll work hard for you, Ms. Porkman. I just need some money so I can eat. I'll take the job.

Porkman: *[skeptically]* Well, you don't look like much, but I guess you'll do. The pay's not much either. You'll feed the pigs and clean up after them too. Now have at it, beggar boy. *[gestures to the pigsty]* There's the pigsty. It's all yours, bless your heart. You'll get paid in a week, if you last that long. *[exits]*

Perez: Thank you—I guess.

[Perez enters the pigsty, picks up five-gallon bucket, and begins tossing dried banana chips around. Enter Iheara Pig, who has been out of view.]

Perez: Here piggy, piggy, piggy. *[throws a chip down; Pig pretends to be interested in it]* Boy, I have to do this for a whole week. And I haven't even cleaned up after them yet. Smells terrible in this pigsty. Oh brother. *[starts examining a banana chip]* If only I could eat these things . . . *[sniffs one]* Matter of fact they smell pretty good. I'm so hungry. And I don't get paid for a week. What am I going to do? Oh boy. *[kneels near Pig, staring]*

Pig: *[looks up indignantly]* I am not!

Perez: *[shocked]* What?

Pig: I am not a boy. I'm a pig.

Perez: What?

Pig: I said, I am not a boy, I'm a pig.

Perez: *[looks up, baffled; thinks lack of food is causing him to lose it]* You're a pig, huh? Great—I'm so hungry, I'm imagining things. I'm actually imagining I hear a pig talking to me.

Pig: At your service, sir. By the way what's *your* name?

Perez: My name? OK, I'll go along with this. My name is Perez. What's your name?

Pig: You already know my name. You said it.

Perez: I did?

Pig: You did. It's Iheara.

Perez: Iheara? I hear a pig?

Pig: *[squeals this line as only a pig could do]* Preee-cisely.

Perez: I'm losing my marbles. This can't be happening. I'm actually talking to a pig named Iheara. I hear a pig. This is totally wacko. This is the last straw. *[holds up banana chip]*

Pig: Actually, it's not a straw—it's a dried banana chip; and can I have it? I'm hungry too, in case you haven't noticed..

Perez: *[believes he has completely lost his mind—jumps up, dumps over the rest of the bucket, and screams]* AHHH-HHHHH . . . I've got to go home! I always had it so good at home—no one ever starved there or went crazy from hunger. What in the world is wrong with me? I can't stay here a minute longer. *[grabs a stick with a satchel attached, starts making his way home]* I'm going home. When I see Dad, I'll tell him I'm so sorry for all the trouble I caused. I'll tell him I did wrong by leaving home. I'll tell him I'll just work in the fields like one of his servants if he'll take me back. Dad was so good to me. And I was so stupid. I'll tell Dad how sorry I am. Maybe he'll let me come home. . . .

[Perez races down one aisle and up the other back toward home. While he is offstage, Dad looks up from his desk and sees him. Dad leaps out of his seat

and runs to him; they meet halfway down an aisle and embrace. Perez gets down on knees and begs.]

Perez: Dad, I'm sorry. I've done wrong. I'm not worthy to be your son. Please forgive me.

Dad: My son, stand up. I forgive you, and we can talk about that later. But right now we have to celebrate. *[shouts offstage]* Phoebe! Bring a ring, bring the best robe, start preparing a meal. We're going to have a feast and celebrate! *[Phoebe enters immediately with ring and robe]* Phoebe, my son has come home again. He was lost and now he's found. Let's celebrate! Come on, son—let's go to the house. I am *so* glad to see you!

[Father and son happily and quickly move past Phoebe, exit side door. Phoebe trails behind. At that moment, Pedro comes up the aisle.]

Pedro: Phoebe, what's all the noise around here? What's going on?

Phoebe: Your brother Perez has returned, and we're having a huge party and celebration. I must go and prepare the food.

Pedro: Go then. *[dismisses her with a wave of the hand; pauses and says angrily]* Of all the dirty tricks! My little brother leaves, takes Dad's money with him, and probably wastes it all, if I know him. And now he's back. Whoopee. Big deal. It's not fair!

Dad: *[has walked up behind Pedro without being seen]* What's not fair, son?

Pedro: Dad! *[surprised but determined to speak his mind]* Dad, all these years I've been slaving away for you and never disobeyed you—not once. And you've never thrown a party for me. Now this no-good brother of mine comes back after wasting all your money. And you throw the party of the century. Is that fair?

Dad: *[puts hand on Philip's shoulder, speaks reassuringly]* Son, as I love you, I also love Perez. And I forgive him. Don't you see—he was as good as dead. He was lost, but now he's found. He's alive. And I forgive him. We *have* to celebrate. Don't you see? I would do the same for you, Pedro. I love you just the same. Now come to the party. Give your brother a hug. Forgive him. Forgive him, Pedro, I beg you. And welcome him home.

[Dad slowly walks away, leaving Pedro staring after him—and leaving the audience not knowing if he did as his father requested or not.]

The Good Samaritan
Based on Luke 10:25-37

Characters (in order of appearance)
Moe (Robber)
Meg (Moe's female accomplice)
Josh (Traveler, a Jewish person who dislikes Samaritans)
Nadab (Priest, someone who usually worked in the temple)
Levi (Levite, a high-ranking and very well dressed religious official, could be female)
Sam (Samaritan traveler)

Suggested Costumes
Costumes can be traditional or contemporary, or a happy blend of both.
Moe and Meg: dark-colored clothing or leather jackets, head-wraps or black cowboy hats
Josh: sandals and glasses, must carry a money bag or wallet
Nadab: simple robe or dark clothing, wears a cross around his neck
Levi: well-dressed, either a bright sash and turban or a suit
Sam: robe and head-wrap or contemporary hiking clothes, carries a Bible

Set and Props
This is a one-scene set—the road from Jerusalem to Jericho (the scene at the inn is not included). If you wish, suggest a path by outlining it with some rocks and plants. You will need something for the two robbers to hide behind—perhaps a couple of folding chairs draped with burlap to resemble a boulder. You'll need a fake rock (costume shop) near the road area, center stage. (Paper shopping bags turned plainside out and stuffed with newspapers or newsprint make good boulders.)

Additional props:
- walking sticks
- canteens, cup
- clean white sock
- money bag or wallet
- watch
- Ace bandage

Set/Synopsis
Thugs Moe and Meg are plotting their next mugging as Josh the Jew is about to pass them. Moe and Meg are hiding (audience can see and hear them—just their heads are visible behind their hiding place). Moe and Meg mug Josh and leave him unconscious beside the road. Nadab the priest comes by. He sees Josh but continues on his journey because he is late for evening prayers. Levi the Levite comes upon Josh and doesn't want to mess up his new (very beautiful) priestly clothes. Finally, Sam the Samaritan comes by and aids his neighbor (who, as a Jew, is traditionally his sworn enemy). Sam cites the biblical principle of loving your neighbor as yourself. He and Josh set off for a nearby inn, with Sam agreeing to foot the bill.

Moe: All right. Sssshhhhhhh. Here he comes. You ready, Meg?

Meg: Ready Moe. Same plan as last time?

Moe: Absolutely. Works like a charm. *[Moe jumps in front of Josh and greets him joyfully; Meg remains hidden]* Well, HELLOOOOO there. How are you, tired traveler? Where are you headed, and what is your name? May I be of assistance to you?

Josh: *[a little scared at first, but then trusting Moe]* W-w-w-well, I'm heading to Jericho from Jerusalem. My name's Josh. And you're right, I am tired. It's hot enough to fry eggs on the rocks! It's a long way to Jericho.

Moe: *[exaggerated concern]* Sure is, Josh. Seventeen miles, to be exact. And a 3,300 foot descent through rocky, desert country. Lots of caves too. Good places for robbers to ambush people like you. I hope you're being very careful, Josh.

Josh: Oh yes, very. Not much gets by me. By the way, you seem to know a lot about this area. Any idea where I could get some water?—I'm out. *[turns empty canteen upside down]*

Moe: *[fake kindness in his voice]* Sure. Here, take a drink of my water from this cup *[pours a cup and passes it to Josh]* while I pour some of my water into your canteen.

[While Moe and Josh have been talking, Meg—hitherto unseen by Josh—has sneaked in behind Josh, on all fours. She is waiting for Moe to give Josh a shove and tumble backwards. Josh starts to drink the water. Moe turns and pretends to be filling Josh's canteen with his water, then gives Josh a shove; Josh falls over Meg. This is sheer, ripsnorting fun for an audience of kids, so play it for all it's worth!]

Meg: *[shouting]* Get him, Moe! Get him! Don't let him get away. Stuff that sock in his mouth, so he can't yell for help. Get his money. Grab his sandals. They're just your size. *[Moe and Meg are doing the mugging activities as they are shouting here.]*

Moe: Right—a perfect fit! *[tries on sandals; it only adds to the humor if they are obviously too large or too small, so don't worry about a precise match]*

Meg: Take his glasses—he'll never find us then.

Moe: Yeah, this poor sap can barely see *with* his glasses.

Meg: We'll sell them in Jericho. All right, we're all set. Just clunk him over the head a few times. Make sure he can't follow us.

[Moe grabs strategically placed fake rock (or club of some sort) and gently clunks Josh on the head several times. Josh is knocked out. He remains sprawled on stage. Suddenly the muggers hear a voice singing. Nadab is approaching and singing.]

Moe: Hey! Someone's coming!

Meg: Let's get outta here! *[They run offstage.]*

[Nadab continues to sing more loudly now so that audience can really hear. He is singing the song "Make Me a Servant." Nadab makes his way and then notices and practically stumbles upon Josh. Nadab is filled with concern.]

Nadab: Oh dear. What have we here? Looks like this poor fellow's been beaten and robbed! *[makes a big deal about checking his watch, showing it to himself and to the audience]* But, oh dear. What shall I do? Look what time it is! Hmmmmmm. I've got evening prayers at seven. If I lend a hand here . . . *[Nadab considers his options]* Do I have time to help? . . . Uhhhh . . . *[deciding]* . . . Nope, I just don't think it's going to work. Besides, I don't think he's hurt that badly, *[turns toward audience]* do you? Maybe he's juuust . . . *[comes up with bright idea]* . . . taking a nap. Sure, that's it. He's taking a nap. I'll tiptoe around this way. So I won't disturb him. *[gestures a "ssshhhh" to the audience; then tiptoes around Josh, brushes off his hands as if he's really done some work and resumes his journey to get to evening prayers on time; resumes singing]* "Make me a servant, humble and meek, Lord let me lift up, those who are weak. And may the prayer of my heart always be . . ." *[song fades as he exits]*

[A new song begins: "They'll Know We Are Christians by Our Love," sung by Levi the Levite. She is taking the same route as Nadab the priest. She almost stumbles over Josh and immediately shows loving concern; soon, however,

loving concern is preempted by clothing concern.]

Levi: Oh my. Look what we have here. This man is hurt. This man has been hit in the head. This man is filthy and has been robbed. This man really needs help! I better help him. *[moves forward to help, then realizes with horror what she is about to do and gasps]* Aaah! What am I doing? These are my brand spanking new priestly duds. I mean, look at me! All these beautiful clothes I bought with my Master Charge. All my beautiful clothes will get filthy if I help this character. *[pauses and moves closer to get a better look at him.]* Hate to say it, but he looks like a rather *shady* character at that. Nope, not today, buddy. Besides— *[picks up Josh's totally limp arm and checks his pulse]* his heart's beating so he'll be OK. *[lets go of Josh's arm and it drops with a thud; she walks down the path, singing loudly, and exits]* "And they'll know we are Christians by our love, by our love, yes, they'll know we are Christians by our love." *[song fades as she exits]*

[A new song begins: "The B-I-B-L-E." Sam the Samaritan is singing; he's the next person to come down the path. He sees Josh and instantly rushes to his aid.]

Sam: Oh, you poor man! Looks like you've been beaten—and robbed too, I'll bet. *[listens to Josh's heart]* His heart's still beating—that's good. But I've got to try to get him to wake up. *[lifts Josh to a sitting position, shakes him gently]* Come on, friend, wake up. Maybe if I try to give him some water . . . *[pretends to give Josh drink from canteen]*

Josh: *[groaning]* Ohhh, it hurts, my head hurts.

Sam: All right, all right—you're going to be OK. I'll take care of you. *[wraps Josh's head with an Ace bandage]*

Josh: Oh, thank you. I was mugged.

Sam: I see that.

Josh: Yeah, two thugs took all my money. Even took my glasses. I can't see who you are.

Sam: I'm Sam the Samaritan.

Josh: *[shocked, almost recoils]* You're a . . . a . . . Samaritan?

Sam: That's me—Sam the Samaritan.

Josh: *[quickly explaining]* But I'm a Jew. We can't stand each other. At least we're not supposed to be able to.

Sam: *[laughs and dismisses it with a wave of his hand]* Oh, that old thing about Jews and Samaritans being bitter enemies? Is that what you're talking about?

Josh: Yeah. That's it.

Sam: Well, I think the Word of God tells us something different than that *[takes out Bible]*

Josh: Oh really? What?

Sam: God wants us to love our neighbor. And our neighbor is *anybody* who needs our help, even if they think we're enemies. *[opens up Bible and shows Josh]* That's what the Scriptures teach us right here. You ought to know that.

Josh: All I know right now is that I'm glad you were kind to me, even though I'm supposed to be your enemy.

Sam: No problem at all. You know what? I don't even know your name.

Josh: I'm Josh the Jew.

Sam: Well, Josh, I'm going to help you get to the nearest inn. It's not far.

Josh: Oh, you just go ahead. You gave me water, you bandaged my head. I'll be all right.

Sam: No way. C'mon! Let's go. You can do it. We'll get there together. I'll help you get to the inn. *[They get up* *and start walking, Josh leaning on Sam for support.]*

Josh: But I don't have any money to pay for the inn. . . . Those thieves took it all. . . .

Sam: Don't worry—I'll pay for the inn. And you can stay as long as you want, until you're completely better.

Josh: I don't know how to thank you. You've been so kind to me.

Sam: Hey, I'm just trying to love my neighbor, like God tells us to do in his Word.

Josh: Well, then, thank God for his Word to us.

Sam: You can say that again. Now let's get you to that inn, my friend. . . . *[They exit slowly, Josh supported by Sam.]*

Ha La La La

Words and music: David Graham
© 1978 C.A. Music (div. of C.A. Records, Inc.). All rights reserved. ASCAP.

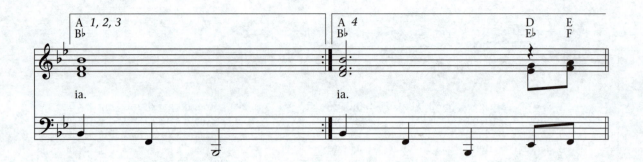

Stop and Let Me Tell You

1 Stop! and let me tell you what the Lord has done for me.
2 Go! and tell the sto-ry of the Christ of Cal-va-ry.
3 Watch! and be— read-y, for the Lord may come to-day.

Stop! and let me tell you what the Lord has done for me. He for-
Go! and tell the sto-ry of the Christ of Cal-va-ry. He'll for-
Watch! and be— read-y, for the Lord may come to-day. He will

gave my sin and he saved my soul, he cleansed my heart and he made me whole.
give their sins, he will save their souls, he'll cleanse their hearts, he will make them whole.
come a-gain in the clouds for me and take me home for e-ter-ni-ty.

Stop! and let me tell you what the Lord has done for me.
Go! and tell the sto-ry of the Christ of Cal-va-ry.
Watch! and be— read-y, for the Lord may come to-day.

Words and music: St. 1-2, unknown; st. 3, Wallace Grant
Music: unknown; arr. Larry Haron
St. 2-3 © 1963 and arr. © 1969, Child Evangelism Fellowship, Inc. (admin. by The Copyright Company, Nashville, TN). All rights reserved. International copyright secured. Used by permission.

He Is the Rock

Words and music: Troy and Genie Nilsson
© 1997 Bridge Building Music (BMI, a division of Brentwood-Benson Music Publishing, Inc.) All rights reserved. Used by permission. Unauthorized duplication prohibited.

The Wise Man and the Foolish Man

Words: adapted from Matthew 7:24-27
Music: Unknown

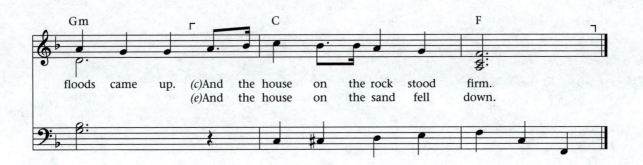

Big House

Words and music: Mark Stuart, Barry Blair, Will McGinniss, Bob Herdman
© 1993 Flicker USA Publishing/Up in The Mix Music/BMI. All rights reserved. Used by permission.

Actions

Come, and go with me
(Motion "Come here," then point to yourself.)

to my Father's house.
(Point up.)

It's a big, big house
(Put fingertips together overhead to suggest the peak of a roof.)

with lots of room.
(Roll your arms in front of you.)

A big, big table
(Spread your arms wide.)

with lots and lots of food.
(Motion as if feeding yourself.)

A big, big yard
(Spread your arms wide.)

where we can play football.
(Pretend to toss a football.)

A big, big house:
(Put fingertips together overhead to suggest the peak of a roof.)

it's my Father's house.
(Point up.)

Amazing Grace/Fill It Up

1. A-mazing grace how sweet the sound that saved a wretch like me!
2. Twas grace that taught my heart to fear, and grace my fears re-lieved;
3. The Lord has prom-ised good to me, has word my hope se-cures;
4. Through man-y dan-gers, toils, and snares I have al-read-y come;
5. When we've been there ten thou-sand years, bright shin-ing as the sun,

I once was lost but now am found, was blind but now I see.
how pre-cious did that grace ap-pear the hour I first be-lieved!
he will my shield and por-tion be as long as life en-dures.
'tis grace hath brought me safe thus far, and grace will lead me home.
we've no less days to sing God's praise than when we'd first be-gun.

Refrain
(So fill it up.) Fill it up and let it o-ver-flow. (So fill it

Words: John Newton 1779
Music: Traditional

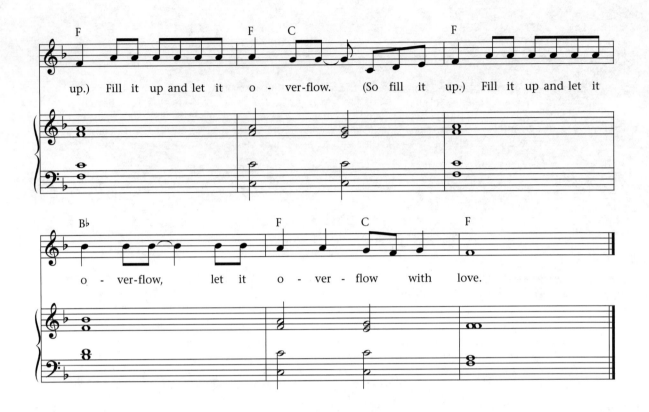

The Great Parade

Words and music: Richard K. Avery and Donald S. Marsh
© 1971, Hope Publishing Co. (Carol Stream, IL 60188). All rights reserved. Used by permission. Contact Hope Publishing Co. for permission to reproduce this hymn (1-800-323-1049).

Always play the Refrain loudly and triumphantly! Play the continued pattern under the reading of the names quietly and mysteriously. Play the instrumental repetitions imaginatively! Let the excitement build. Improvise at will and have a marvelous time! Add some names from your own church.

Jesu, Jesu, Fill Us with Your Love

Words: Tom Colvin
Music: Ghana folk song, adapt. Tom Colvin; arr. Jane Marshall
Words © 1969, Hope Publishing Co.
Music © 1969 and this arr. © 1982, Hope Publishing Co. (Carol Stream, IL 60188). All rights reserved. Used by permission. Contact Hope Publishing Co. for permission to reproduce this hymn (1-800-323-1049).

The Good Samaritan

Words and music: Mary Lu Walker
© 1998 by Mary Lu Walker, 16 Brown Road, Corning, New York 14830

Tell It!

Words and music: Cindy Berry
© 1997 Van Ness Press, Inc. All rights reserved. Used by permission.

Two Houses

Sandy Land

Words and music: Karen Lafferty
© 1981 Maranatha Praise, Inc. (admin. by The Copyright Company, Nashville, TN). All rights reserved. International copyright secured. Used by permission.

You Shall Love the Lord

Words: Matthew 22:37-39, NKJV
Music: Frank Hernandez

© 1990 Birdwing Music (ASCAP). All rights controlled and administered by The Sparrow Corp., P.O. Box 2120, Chatsworth, CA 91311. All rights reserved. International copyright secured.

Make Me a Servant

Words and music: Kelly Willard
© 1982 CCCM Music/Willing Heart Music (Admin. by Maranatha! Music c/o The Copyright Company, Nashville, TN). All rights reserved. International copyright secured. Used by permission.

Memory Fun

Your word is a lamp to my feet and a light for my path.

—Psalm 119:105, NIV

Memory Fun

Your word is a lamp to my feet and a light for my path.

—Psalm 119:105, NIV

Memory Fun

Your word is a lamp to my feet and a light for my path.

—Psalm 119:105, NIV

Memory Fun

Your word is a lamp to my feet and a light to my path.

—Psalm 119:105, NRSV

Memory Fun

Your word is a lamp to my feet and a light to my path.

—Psalm 119:105, NRSV

Memory Fun

Your word is a lamp to my feet and a light to my path.

—Psalm 119:105, NRSV

Memory Challenge

24"Therefore everyone who hears these words of mine and puts them into practice is like a wise man who built his house on the rock.

25The rain came down, the streams rose, and the winds blew and beat against that house; yet it did not fall, because it had its foundation on the rock.

26But everyone who hears these words of mine and does not put them into practice is like a foolish man who built his house on sand.

27The rain came down, the streams rose, and the winds blew and beat against that house, and it fell with a great crash."

—Matthew 7:24-27, NIV

Memory Challenge

24"Therefore everyone who hears these words of mine and puts them into practice is like a wise man who built his house on the rock.

25The rain came down, the streams rose, and the winds blew and beat against that house; yet it did not fall, because it had its foundation on the rock.

26But everyone who hears these words of mine and does not put them into practice is like a foolish man who built his house on sand.

27The rain came down, the streams rose, and the winds blew and beat against that house, and it fell with a great crash."

—Matthew 7:24-27, NIV

Memory Challenge

²⁴"Everyone then who hears these words of mine and acts on them will be like a wise man who built his house on rock.

²⁵The rain fell, the floods came, and the winds blew and beat on that house, but it did not fall, because it had been founded on rock.

²⁶And everyone who hears these words of mine and does not act on them will be like a foolish man who built his house on sand.

²⁷The rain fell, and the floods came, and the winds blew and beat against that house, and it fell—and great was its fall!"

—Matthew 7:24-27, NRSV

Memory Challenge

²⁴"Everyone then who hears these words of mine and acts on them will be like a wise man who built his house on rock.

²⁵The rain fell, the floods came, and the winds blew and beat on that house, but it did not fall, because it had been founded on rock.

²⁶And everyone who hears these words of mine and does not act on them will be like a foolish man who built his house on sand.

²⁷The rain fell, and the floods came, and the winds blew and beat against that house, and it fell—and great was its fall!"

—Matthew 7:24-27, NRSV

A farmer went out to sow (plant) his seed.

Still other seed fell on good soil. It produced a crop 100, 60, or 30 times more than what was planted.

Think About It

Why did the farmer scatter so many seeds?

Which place is the best for seeds to fall?

Which places are not good for seeds?

Just as the farmer scattered MANY seeds, God wants MANY people to be in his kingdom. Talk with your family about some ways we can help spread the good news about Jesus.

The Parable of the Sower and the Seeds
(Matthew 13:3-8)

Name: _____

Walk With Me curriculum, © 2004, CRC Publications. Permission granted to photocopy this page for classroom use.

Other seeds fell on rocky places without much soil. The plants sprang up quickly because the soil was shallow. But when the sun came up, it burned the plants. They dried up because they had no roots.

Other seeds fell among thorns. The thorns grew up and choked the plants.

As the farmer sowed, some seeds fell on the path. The birds came and ate them up.

Where Am I in This Parable?

Use one or more of these sentence starters to write about how you see yourself in the parable of the sower and the seed.

- I'm kind of like a seed that's been planted somewhere, but I'm just not sure where at the moment. I really like to . . .

- I'm kind of like a plant that's growing pretty well but I've got to fight off some thorns in my life, thorns like . . .

- I've got a long way to go, but I think I'm like the seed that landed on good soil and is growing into a healthy plant. I hope that . . .

- I'd really like to be more like that farmer, showing and telling others the good news about Jesus. One way I think I can do that is by . . .

- I really can't find myself anywhere in this parable. Here's the way I'd describe my own relationship with Jesus . . .

Walk With Me curriculum, © 2004, CRC Publications. Permission granted to photocopy this page for classroom use.

The Parable of the Wise and Foolish Builders
(Matthew 7:24-27)

Name: _____

Crowds of people followed Jesus everywhere to hear the good news of the kingdom. Jesus told them this story—called a parable—about two builders. One was wise and one was foolish (not wise!).

When Jesus was done telling this story, the people were amazed at his teaching. We also need to listen to and do what Jesus says. That's the way to be wise!

Think About It

Which builder was wise? Which builder was foolish?

If we listen to Jesus and do what he says, we are like the builder who _____.

If we hear what Jesus says but don't do it, we are like the builder who _____.

How can we find out what Jesus wants us to do?

What are some things that Jesus tells us to do?

With Me curriculum, © 2004, CRC Publications. Permission granted to photocopy this for classroom use.

Jesus said, "Everyone who listens to me and does what I say is like a wise man who built his house on the rock."

rain came down and the water came up. The wind w and beat against that house. But the house did fall because it was built on the rock.

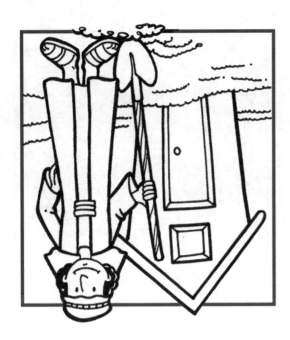

Everyone who hears what I say but does not do what I say is like a foolish man who built his house on sand.

The rain came down and the water came up. The wind blew and beat against that house. And the house fell down with a great crash!

House Pattern

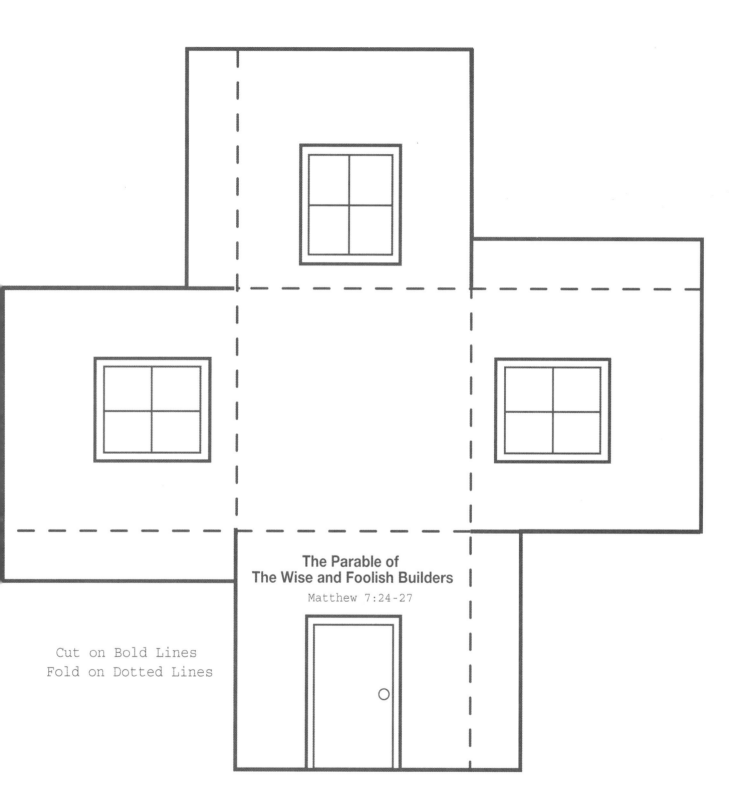

Roof Pattern

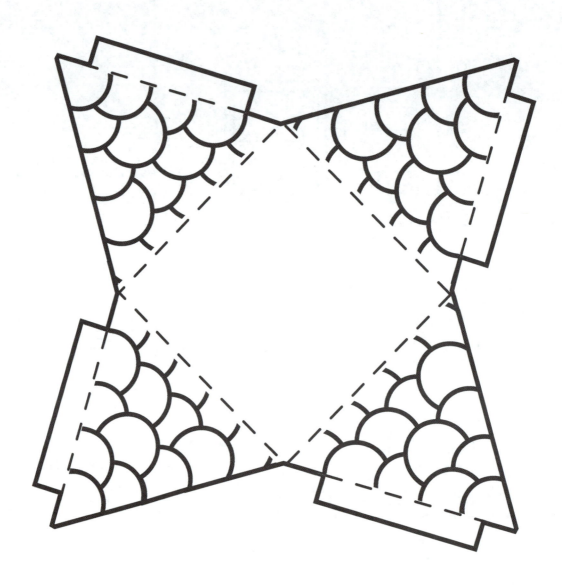

Cut on Bold Lines
Fold on Dotted Lines

Builder Pattern

Same Story, Different Versions—Matthew 7:24-29

New International Version

"Therefore everyone who hears these words of mine and puts them into practice is like a wise man who built his house on the rock. The rain came down, the streams rose, and the winds blew and beat against that house; yet it did not fall, because it had its foundation on the rock. But everyone who hears these words of mine and does not put them into practice is like a foolish man who built his house on sand. The rain came down, the streams rose, and the winds blew and beat against that house, and it fell with a great crash."

When Jesus had finished saying these things, the crowds were amazed at his teaching, because he taught as one who had authority, and not as their teachers of the law.

The Message

"These words I speak to you are not incidental additions to your life, homeowner improvements to your standard of living. They are foundational words, words to build a life on. If you work these words into your life, you are like a smart carpenter who built his house on solid rock. Rain poured down, the river flooded, a tornado hit—but nothing moved that house. It was fixed to the rock.

"But if you just use my words in Bible studies and don't work them into your life, you are like a stupid carpenter who built his house on the sandy beach. When a storm rolled in and the waves came up, it collapsed like a house of cards."

When Jesus concluded his address, the crowd burst into applause. They had never heard teaching like this. It was apparent that he was living everything he was saying—quite a contrast to their religion teachers! This was the best teaching they had ever heard.

King James Version

Therefore whosoever heareth these sayings of mine, and doeth them, I will liken him unto a wise man, which built his house upon a rock:

And the rain descended, and the floods came, and the winds blew, and beat upon that house; and it fell not: for it was founded upon a rock.

And every one that heareth these sayings of mine, and doeth them not, shall be likened unto a foolish man, which built his house upon the sand:

And the rain descended, and the floods came, and the winds blew, and beat upon that house; and it fell: and great was the fall of it.

And it came to pass, when Jesus had ended these sayings, the people were astonished at his doctrine:

For he taught them as one having authority, and not as the scribes.

New Living Translation

"Anyone who listens to my teaching and obeys me is wise, like a person who builds a house on solid rock. Though the rain comes in torrents and the floodwaters rise and the winds beat against that house, it won't collapse, because it is built on rock. But anyone who hears my teaching and ignores it is foolish, like a person who builds a house on sand. When the rains and floods come and the winds beat against that house, it will fall with a mighty crash."

After Jesus finished speaking, the crowds were amazed at his teaching, for he taught as one who had real authority—quite unlike the teachers of religious law.

SMALL GROUP 4-8
YEAR 1 SUMMER SESSION 2

Survey: Where Am I in this Parable?

Try this multiple-choice quiz to discover how you see yourself in the parable of the wise and foolish builders.

1. When I think about listening to Jesus . . .

    __ Sometimes I could use a good hearing aid.
    __ I can hear the words, but they don't mean much to me and the way I live.
    __ I'm learning to listen because I know that Jesus wants the very best for me.
    __ Other: _____.

2. Right now, in my life, the most important ways I see and hear Jesus are

    __ when I read my Bible.
    __ when I pray.
    __ when I'm with friends who are Christians.
    __ from my mom or dad.
    __ from an older brother or sister.
    __ from a Christian teacher.
    __ in church.
    __ Other: _____.

3. When it comes to *knowing* what God and Jesus want me to do, I'm

    __ mostly in the dark.
    __ fuzzy on the details.
    __ pretty clear on most everything.
    __ Other: _____.

4. When it comes to hearing *and* doing what Jesus wants me to do,

    __ I'm building my house on the Rock.
    __ I'm building my house on the sand.
    __ sometimes I'm building on the rock, sometimes on the sand.
    __ I've got this "doing" bit down cold.
    __ I could use some help in practicing what I know is right.
    __ Other: _____.

5. One thing that helps me *do* what I know is right is . . .

6. If Jesus himself had just told me this parable about the two builders, and if he and I were in a room all by ourselves, this is what he might say to me:

    And this is what I might say to him:

The Parable of the Great Banquet
(Luke 14:15-24)

Name: _____

A certain man was preparing a great banquet. He invited many guests. When everything was ready, he sent his servant to tell the guests to come.

"I tell you, not one of those people I first invited will get a taste of my banquet."

Think About It

Why didn't the people want to come to the banquet?

How do you think the person who gave the banquet felt when no one wanted to come?

What kind of people finally came to the banquet?

What kind of people does God invite to come to his banquet and be part of his family?

Walk With Me curriculum, © 2004, CRC Publications. Permission granted to photocopy this page for classroom use.

But they all made excuses. They were all busy with other things. "No, we can't come," they said.

Then the master told his servant, "Go out to the roads and country lanes. Tell everyone to come! I want my house to be full."

Where Am I in This Parable?

God has invited *you* to come to be part of his family. One day you will enjoy being with God and with all other believers from every time and place and nation and tribe. Use one or more of these sentence starters to write about how you see yourself responding to God's invitation in the parable of the great banquet.

- I've not gotten around to opening up God's invitation just yet because . . .

- I've heard God's invitation, and right now I'm seriously thinking about . . .

- I've heard God's invitation, but, like those three guys in the parable, I have to say no. You see, I have this really good excuse . . .

- I'm one of those "on the street" whom God invited to the banquet after the others said no. I said yes to God's invitation. What this means for my life is . . .

- I really can't find myself anywhere in this parable. Here's the way I'd describe my own relationship with Jesus . . .

Story Sequencing Cards

The Parable of the Great Banquet

Read Luke 14:15-24. Draw a picture on each of the story cards that illustrates what's written on the card. Color the pictures and cut out the cards. Then mix up the cards and put them back in order as you retell the parable.

A certain man was preparing a great banquet and invited many guests.

"Come. Everything is ready."

"I can't come. I just bought a field, and I must go and see it."

"I can't come. I just bought five teams of oxen, and I want to try them out."

"I can't come. I just got married."

The owner of the house became angry. "Go into the town and bring in people who are poor, who can't see, who can't walk."

"What you have ordered has been done, but there is still room."

"Go out to the roads and country lanes and make them come in, so that my banquet hall will be full."

The Parable of the Lost Son
(Luke 15:11-32)

A man had two sons. The younger one said, "Father, give me my share of the family money."

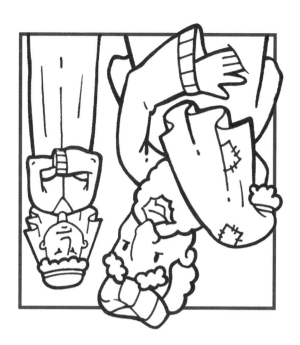

The son said, "Father, I have sinned. I am no longer worthy to be called your son." But the father forgave him and said, "Let's have a feast to celebrate! For this son of mine was lost and is found." But this made the older brother angry.

Think About It

What did the son do that was wrong?

How did the father show that he loved and forgave his son?

When we do something wrong and we tell God we are sorry, what does God do?

What does God want us to do when someone does something mean or unkind to us?

With Me curriculum, © 2004, CRC Publications. Permission granted to photocopy this for classroom use.

Name: _____

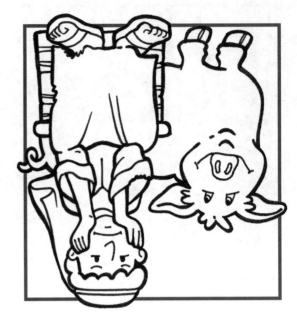

At last, poor and hungry, he decided to go home, where there was plenty of food. "I will tell my father I am sorry and ask for a job," he thought. So he began the long walk home.

found a job feeding pigs. He was so hungry wanted to eat the pigs' food. But no one gave anything.

His father saw him coming. He was filled with love for his son. He ran to meet him, hugged him, and kissed him.

Then the younger son left home for a faraway land. He wasted all his money. He became very poor and very hungry.

Story Card

**The Parable of the Lost Son
(Luke 15:11-32)**

1. A man had two sons. The younger son wanted to leave home. He asked his father for his share of the family money.

2. He left home for a country far away. There he spent all his money on foolish things.

3. When he ran out of money, he found a job feeding pigs. He was so hungry he wanted to eat the pigs' food. No one gave him anything.

4. At last he decided to go home, where there was plenty of food. "I will tell my father I am sorry and ask for a job," he thought. So he began the long walk home.

5. His father saw him coming down the road. He was filled with love for his son. He ran to meet him and hugged him!

6. The father forgave him and gave him a big party. He treated him like a son, not a servant.

7. The older son was jealous. He refused to go to the party. The father begged him to come and said, "Everything I have is yours. But we have to celebrate and be glad. This brother of yours was lost. And now he is found!"

What does this parable mean?
Like the father in the story, God accepts us and forgives us. He wants us to accept and forgive others.

Where Am I in This Parable?

Use all of these sentence starters to write about what the parable of the lost son means to you..

- Like the younger brother in this parable, I am someone who sometimes . . .

- Like the father in this parable, God is someone who . . .

- When God forgives me for something I've done wrong, I feel . . .

- When it comes to accepting and forgiving others as God wants me to do, I

    ____ am sometimes like the older brother—slow to forgive and accept others.
    ____ generally do OK. I think of myself as an accepting and forgiving person.

- One person that I know God wants me to forgive and/or be accepting of is _____. I will try to do so by . . .

Once there was a man who asked Jesus a question: "Who is my neighbor?" To teach us who our neighbors are, Jesus told this story.

Then he put the man on his own donkey. He took him to an inn, and took care of him. Jesus said, "This is the way I want you to be."

Think About It

How do you think the man who was hurt felt when the priest and the Levite walked right past him?

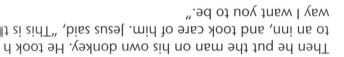

How did the Samaritan help him?

How do you think he felt when the Samaritan helped him?

How can we be a neighbor to people around us?

The Parable of the Good Samaritan
(Luke 10:25-37)

Name: _____

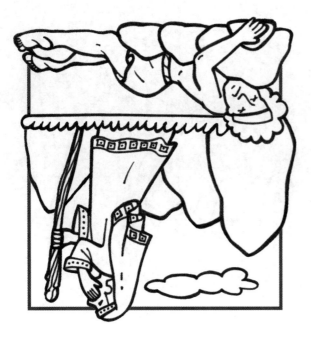

A priest was going down the same road. When he saw the man, he passed by on other side.

A Levite also came by. When he saw the man, he passed by on the other side too.

Then along came a Samaritan—a person whom most Jews, like the wounded man, did not like. The Samaritan saw the wounded man and felt sorry for him. He took care of the man.

A man was walking from Jerusalem to Jericho. Robbers attacked him. They stripped him of his clothes, beat him, and left him half dead.

Good Samaritan Puppets and Story Card

The Good Samaritan

The Good Samaritan

The Good Samaritan (Luke 10:25-37)

Jesus told a story about a man who was beaten and robbed. The robbers left him by the side of the road. Three people came down the road and had a chance to help the man who was hurt:

1. A priest—he passed by on the other side of the road.
2. A Levite—he passed by on the other side too!
3. A Samaritan—he took care of the man's wounds, brought him to an inn, and paid for his care.

What does this parable mean for us?

The Jews and Samaritans usually hated each other. But this Samaritan was kind to a Jew. Jesus wants us to be neighbors to everyone. He wants us to help others and show God's love to everyone.

The Robber

The Priest

The Levite

The Innkeeper

Neighborly Situations

Read the role-play situation (below) that you've been asked to do. With one or two partners, act out two different endings:

(1) Act out an ending in which you give excuses for *not* being a good neighbor in this situation.
(2) Act out an ending that shows how to be a good neighbor in this situation.

1. There's a new kid at school who's kind of shy. Other kids sometimes laugh and poke fun of this person. One day you're eating your lunch and the new kid asks if he can sit with you. You're sitting at a table with a friend who doesn't like the new kid. You . . .

2. You are on your way home in the school bus. There's a kid in grade 3 who rides the bus and is often picked on by a bully who's your age. Today, the bully is being especially mean, pushing and shoving and hurting the younger kid. You see it happening, so you . . .

3. Sometimes your friends say bad things about this kid because she comes from a different country. Stuff like, "She's so stupid she can't even speak English right." One day they start saying things like that in front of you. You . . .

4. One kid in your class wears uncool clothes that are probably from the mission store. Some of your friends call this kid "Rags" and other mean names. One day your mom suggests that you invite this uncool kid over for supper and a movie. You . . .

5. A friend has betrayed you by telling kids at school something that you told your friend in secret. Other kids are looking at you and laughing because they know this secret. That night your friend comes over. "I'm really sorry I told your secret," the friend says. "Can we still be friends?" You . . .

6. Your dad asks you to spend your Saturday morning raking your neighbor's leaves. "He's too old to do it himself," your dad says. The trouble is, you've already told a friend you'd be over on Saturday. Besides, the old man next door is kind of crabby; he acts like he doesn't like kids. You . . .

7. You're riding on the city bus when a homeless person gets on and sits down right next to you. She's wearing a heavy, dirty coat, even though it's summer, and it's obvious she hasn't had a shower for quite some time. She starts mumbling to herself and then, all of a sudden, she starts talking to you. You . . .

8. Invent your own situation:

Where Am I in This Parable?

Use two or more of these sentence starters to write about what the parable of the good Samaritan means to you.

- Like the robbers, I sometimes sometimes beat other people down by . . .

- Like the victim, I too am sometimes hurt by others when they . . .

- Like the priest or the Levite, sometimes I fail to be a good neighbor when I . . .

- Like the Samaritan, I have taken time out to help others; for example, I . . .

Leader's Evaluation

We invite you to take a few minutes to tell us how *Walk With Me* is working for you. Please complete this form and return it to

WWM Evaluation
Kindergarten-Grade 8
Summer, Book 1
Faith Alive Christian Resources
2850 Kalamazoo Ave. SE
Grand Rapids, MI 49560

 Save time by e-mailing your comments to us at
editors@WalkWithMeOnline.org
Be sure to tell us that you are teaching Summer, Book 1.

Things I found especially helpful/effective in these materials . . .

Things I changed or supplemented in this unit . . .

Joys/challenges I encountered while teaching this unit . . .

Name:

Church/Denomination:

Grade level I teach:

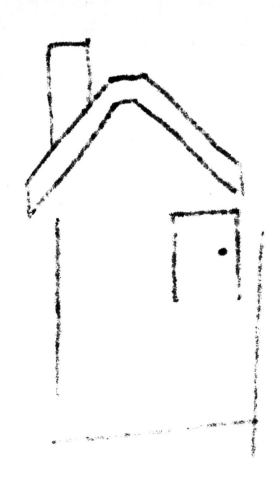